MAGREY

The CHRISTMAS LETTERS

Celebrating Advent
with THOSE WHO TOLD THE STORY FIRST

ABINGDON PRESS | NASHVILLE

The Christmas Letters
Celebrating Advent with Those Who Told the Story First

Library of Congress Control Number: 2024937326
978-1-7910-3323-1

MANUFACTURED IN THE
UNITED STATES OF AMERICA

For Maddy and Grace

The Christmas Letters

Celebrating Advent with Those Who Told the Story First

The Christmas Letters

978-1-7910-3323-1

978-1-7910-3325-5 eBook

The Christmas Letters: DVD

978-1-7910-3327-9

The Christmas Letters: Leader Guide

978-1-7910-3324-8

978-1-7910-3326-2 eBook

Also by Magrey R. deVega

Awaiting the Already:
An Advent Journey Through the Gospels

The Bible Year:
A Journey Through Scripture in 365 Days

Embracing the Uncertain:
A Lenten Study for Unsteady Times

Questions Jesus Asked:
A Six-Week Study in the Gospels

Savior:
What the Bible Says about the Cross

With April Casperson, Ingrid McIntyre, and Matt Rawle
Almost Christmas:
A Wesleyan Advent Experience

CONTENTS

INTRODUCTION

Each year, most of us share in the ritual of sending and receiving Christmas cards. These cards typically contain more than just the commensurate "Merry Christmas!" greeting and a signature from the sender. Often, they contain photos of the family, highlights of their past year, and words of greeting to family and friends. Sometimes, they even include letters, folded and tucked into the envelope.

Even though the sending of Christmas cards has been around since the mid-nineteenth century, I'm not sure how or when the tradition of including personal letters began. No other time of year offers such an occasion; not Easter, or New Year's Day, or Thanksgiving. Somehow, we have taken to Christmas to be the time of reflecting, catching up, and looking ahead.

Think about the Christmas letters you have received in the past. You scan the photos to see the places your friends have visited. You read the milestone moments they have observed together. You think about your own interactions with them over the past year. You ponder when you might see them again in person.

These letters are more than news updates or points of reconnection with your family and friends. They are an invitation for their story to intersect with your own, and for your remembrances of them to come alive even for a brief moment in time. You remember what these people have meant to you over the years. You celebrate that, even though you may be separated by distance, you are still connected to one another in kinship and love.

Christmas is the perfect time to reawaken relationships, remember past connections, and ponder the wonder of love that holds us all together.

Now imagine that, tucked among the piles of Christmas letters from family and friends, there waits for you a stack of correspondence from the greatest sender of all: the God who created you, loves you, and draws near to you in Jesus. Wouldn't those be letters worth cherishing?

This study centers on a special set of letters that were delivered thousands of years ago to the earliest Christian communities in the first-century Greco-Roman world. They were not Christmas letters, but they were letters about Jesus. They were not specifically about his birth, but they give us the earliest glimpses about what the church believed about the Incarnation—the miracle that God became human.

Some of these letters were written just decades after Jesus was on earth, even while the Gospel accounts were still circulating in oral form before they were written down. All of them represent faithful attempts by the early church to understand who Jesus was and what his life meant for humankind. To read them now, in the light of Advent and Christmas, is to read them as a kind of Christmas letter to the modern-day church, catching us up on how our spiritual ancestors were opening up to the wonder and power of Jesus Christ.

This study will focus on four Epistles in particular, and we will discover what they reveal to us about what the first Christians believed about the Incarnation. We will see their points of connection to more familiar Advent Scriptures: lectionary texts from the Prophets and the birth narratives in the Gospels.

In chapter 1, we'll look at Romans, particularly the first chapter, and see how Paul's view of Jesus is rooted in the words of the ancient prophets, just as many of the Gospels' birth narratives are rooted in Isaiah. We'll see how Advent prompts us to look back at our own spiritual journey, which will guide us in looking forward to the life God intends for us.

In chapter 2, we'll look at the First Epistle of John, which is connected theologically and literarily with the Gospel of John. We'll see how the famous text from John 1, so often read at Christmas, resonates with 1 John, and how they both point to the Creation arc in Genesis 1. Taken together, they will remind us of how God's love has been revealed throughout salvation history, and is revealed to us in Jesus.

In chapter 3, we'll look at Paul's Letter to the Philippians, including the ancient Christian hymn in the second chapter. We'll explore how that magnificent Scripture gives us a glimpse into the church's earliest views of the Incarnation. Jesus became fully human, fully obedient, and he models for us how to have a mindset of servanthood. We'll connect that to the story of Mary, a standard feature of the third week of Advent, and see how her life exemplifies joyful obedience and service to God.

In chapter 4, we'll conclude our journey with Paul's Letter to the Colossians, which reminds us in the first chapter of

Jesus's full divinity, existing since the days of Creation. When we see Jesus, we see the fullness of God revealed to us, and remember how Jesus is greater than all earthly powers. We'll connect that notion of Christ's full divinity with Matthew's birth narrative, in which Herod saw Jesus as a divine threat to his throne and the Greco-Roman belief in other gods. Most of all, we will be invited to experience the awe and wonder of the Incarnation every day.

So consider these texts as a special set of Christmas letters, written by our spiritual ancestors and inspired by the God who became flesh for us in Jesus. As we read them, we will see our stories intersect with theirs. Though we are separated by time and distance from the earliest Christians, we will celebrate our kinship as fellow believers, and discover how they began to formulate the very beliefs in Jesus that we have inherited over the generations. Most of all, we will rediscover how to make Christmas more than just an annual observance, but a way of life, modeled after Jesus, all year round.

Blessings on the journey!

CHAPTER 1

GOOD NEWS

Looking Back to Look Ahead

CHAPTER 1

GOOD NEWS

Looking Back
to Look Ahead

*From Paul, a slave of Christ Jesus, called to be an apostle
and set apart for God's good news. God promised this good
news about God's Son ahead of time through the prophets in
the Holy Scriptures. His Son was descended from David. He
was publicly identified as God's Son with power through his
resurrection from the dead, which was based on the Spirit
of holiness. This Son is Jesus Christ our Lord. Through him
we have received God's grace and our appointment to be
apostles. This was to bring all Gentiles to faithful obedience
for his name's sake. You who are called by Jesus Christ are
also included among these Gentiles.*

*To those in Rome who are dearly loved by God and called to
be God's people.*

*Grace to you and peace from God our Father and the Lord
Jesus Christ.*

(Romans 1:1-7)

Because Advent is the beginning of the Christian liturgical year, it is appropriate to spend time reflecting on the past year. It begins in the wake of Thanksgiving, when we gather with family and friends to take an inventory of the blessings we have experienced. It ends on the brink of a new calendar year, as we ponder the highs and lows of the past twelve months in anticipation of what lies ahead. Advent prompts us to consider how we have experienced God in the past, and what we long for in the future.

In his book *What We Owe the Future*, William MacAskill describes how the Aymara people of Bolivia and Peru think about time. When you and I envision the past and the future, we see the past as behind us, and the future as ahead of us. Most people and cultures think of the future and past this way, but not the Aymara. They picture the future behind them, and the past as ahead of them.

Why is that? Well, they recognize that the past is the only thing we can see clearly, whereas the future is unforeseeable. So when they picture the past, they point ahead of them. When they think about the future, they point their thumbs behind them. The Aymara believe that in a way, all of us are walking backward into the future.

This is an interesting way to think about Advent. We know what the last year has brought us. And while we begin this journey toward Christmas with some preset ideas on what it will bring—family gatherings, gift exchanges, worship services with carols and candles—we don't *really* know what moments of serendipity or wrestling it will bring. All we know is what we are longing for, and hoping for, based on what we have already experienced.

Take a moment, at the start of this season and the start of this study, to reflect on this stage of your life. What burdens are you carrying into Advent this year?

How is your family? What joys did you celebrate and what hardships still linger?

How is your career? Is your job bringing you satisfaction, and more than a means toward making a living? If you are unemployed, what have you discovered about yourself? If you are retired, what new passions and talents are being kindled?

How is your view of the world? Are you more fearful or hopeful about where the human story is heading? What major events in your community or country are you praying through the most? What do you wish was different about the world today?

How is your mind and heart? What set of words would most describe what you are feeling? Is it peaceful and centered? Troubled or unsettled? My friend Ken Carter, resident bishop of the Western North Carolina Conference of The United Methodist Church, has reminded pastors that generally speaking, people operate—even subconsciously—on the basis of two primary emotional foundations: grief and fear.

Grief is based on what we have lost in the past. Fear is based on what we may lose in the future. Both of these deal with loss, the realized and the possible. Oftentimes, both of those feelings are operating in us at once, capturing us in a kind of intrapsychic tug-of-war that pulls us away from staying in the present.

And then there is your spiritual life. As John Wesley commonly asked, "How is it with your soul?" Are you more like Jesus now than you were this time last year? What advances in your spiritual maturity are you most pleased with? How did you grow in your faith, despite the hardships? What temptations have you struggled with the most? What choices did you make that were less than ideal for a follower of Jesus?

Reflecting on these questions is a helpful and important place to start in this Advent journey. Before we read any of these Epistles and connect their themes to the birth narratives in the Gospels, take some time to reflect on this past year, and what you are longing for as you enter this season.

EVERY FIVE YEARS

I had a therapist many years ago tell me that in her experience with clients, she observed this to be true: every five years, a person's situation in life changes considerably. These changes are often unpredictable, and they can affect numerous aspects of a person's life. It is very common for a person to be in a stage or situation of life now that is very different from where they were five years ago, ten years ago, fifteen years ago, and so on.

Think about that for yourself. In what way is life now different for you than five years in the past, and every multiple of five years before that? Chances are good that life has changed considerably for you. Maybe it has been a change in your residence, your family dynamics, your occupation, your ideological perspective, your health, or any of a number of other factors.

REFLECTION QUESTIONS

1. What highs and lows have defined this past year for you?

2. What burdens are you carrying related to your family, your career, and your stage in life?

3. How is your soul? In what ways have you grown? What sins most cause you to stumble?

This is all to say that no matter what you are facing right now, chances are just as good that you will move past it and through it five years from now. This is not to say that everything in your life will be easier. The struggles of your present moment may be long gone five years from now, but there may be other challenges ahead. And there will be surprising blessings in store for you that you cannot expect now. Life is not static, and no one stays the same. We are simply, as the Aymara would say, walking backward into the future.

This reflection on our past is not only a helpful entry point into the season of Advent; it is a good way to approach the Book of Romans, the first epistle in our journey together.

ROOTED IN THE PAST

Paul's Letter to the Romans is unique in that it is the only epistle he wrote to a community he had not yet visited or established personally. As a result, it contains far fewer references to particular members of the community, or specific issues dividing it, than what is found in other letters.

By the time he wrote the letter, sometime in AD 57–59, the gospel had already reached Rome. Some of its citizens had started to become followers of Jesus Christ and form a Christian community. This epistle, like all of Paul's letters, was written within mere decades after the life and resurrection of Jesus, still within a generation of eyewitnesses to Jesus's ministry on earth. They had heard the stories of Jesus; maybe some had even seen Jesus for themselves. But the faith of the Christian church was still being formed. They still needed to know *what* to believe about Jesus, and *why*.

So we might imagine that for Paul, this letter was not just his way of introducing himself to those early Christians; more important, he wanted to share with them his core convictions about the way of Jesus.

That's why it's interesting that in order to move people forward in developing their beliefs about Jesus, Paul began by reminding them of the past:

> *From Paul, a slave of Christ Jesus, called to be an apostle and set apart for God's good news. God promised this good news about his Son ahead of time through his prophets in the holy scriptures. His Son was descended from David.*
>
> *(Romans 1:1-3)*

Right out of the gate, Paul introduces himself as little more than a servant of Jesus. It is less important to him that the Romans get to know him than they need to get to know the one who sent him. He is just an apostle—a follower, an acolyte, a messenger, not the leader himself. He has been set apart by God to share nothing less than the good news about Jesus Christ.

That's it for introductions. That's all Paul really wants to say about himself. Just 1 verse out of 433. That's enough. Because Paul now really wants to get to the really important part, about introducing people to Jesus.

And how does he want to begin talking about Jesus? By looking at the past:

> *"God promised this good news about his Son ahead of time through his prophets in the holy scriptures."*

> *"His Son was descended from David."*

Let's take each of these one at a time.

UNDERSTANDING THE INCARNATION
THROUGH THE PROPHETS

To understand the meaning and purpose of the Incarnation, we need to begin by looking at the testimony of the Hebrew prophets. It is no surprise that in the Christian lectionary—the ecumenical reference guide of Sunday Scripture texts for worship—the first Sunday of Advent always points us to prophetic texts. The Old Testament readings are from Isaiah or Jeremiah, and the Gospel readings are prophetic in nature, about interpreting the signs of the inbreaking of God into the world.

Paul quotes or paraphrases the prophets over twenty times in Romans, including references to Habakkuk, Malachi, Hosea, and Jeremiah. By far, Paul cites the words of Isaiah, referencing him nineteen times in his Letter to the Romans.

Why was this important to Paul? Because he viewed the arrival of Jesus in the world not as some spontaneous, surprising event, but one that had been anticipated and longed for by generations before him, and planned by God since the beginning. Like a good preacher, he solidifies his argument by referencing sources that would have been familiar to his audience, particularly Christians whose spiritual heritage included the Hebrew tradition.

Of all the Major and Minor Prophets that compose the Hebrew canon, no writer stood taller or spoke more prolifically than Isaiah. He spoke words of comfort and challenge to the Southern Kingdom of Judea in the eighth century BC, confronting the people and their kings for their wayward behavior. Isaiah inspired a prophetic tradition that went beyond the prophet's life, carrying his message forward to later times and circumstances. The book that bears Isaiah's name warned Judah of the coming destruction by the Babylonian Empire. While Judah was in exile, Isaiah gave them words of hope, encouraging them to maintain their commitment to God, who would bring them a deliverer and return them to their land.

Isaiah gives us some of the most vivid imagery related to the messianic promise. Among the nineteen times Paul quotes Isaiah, two are especially relevant for the season of Advent:

Proclaiming the Good News of the Messiah

From Romans 10:15: "And how can they preach unless they are sent? As it is written, *How beautiful are the feet of those who announce the good news.*"

Here is the original text from Isaiah 52:7:

"How beautiful upon the mountains
are the feet of a messenger
who proclaims peace,
who brings good news, who proclaims salvation,
who says to Zion, 'Your God rules!'"

The Historical Lineage of the Messiah

From Romans 15:12:

"And again, Isaiah says,

There will be a root of Jesse,
who will also rise to rule the Gentiles.
The Gentiles will place their hope in him."

Here is the original text from Isaiah 11:10: "On that day, the root of Jesse will stand as a signal to the peoples. The nations will seek him out, and his dwelling will be glorious."

In quoting Isaiah throughout his epistle, Paul was interpreting the conditions of his times in the broader context of history. As Mark Twain is reputed to have once quipped, "History doesn't repeat itself, but it often rhymes." The longing by the people of Judah for deliverance from exile echoed the longing of the Jewish people for liberation from the Roman Empire. The words of the prophets, particularly Isaiah, can capture our own desire today for deliverance from sin, injustice, and other forms of oppression and suffering in our world.

It is in that spirit that the lectionary leans heavily on Isaiah during Advent every year.

Consider these texts from Isaiah we hear all throughout this season:

> *God will judge between the nations,*
> *and settle disputes of mighty nations.*
> *Then they will beat their swords into iron plows*
> *and their spears into pruning tools.*
> *Nation will not take up sword against nation;*
> *they will no longer learn how to make war.*
> *(Isaiah 2:4)*

> *A shoot will grow up from the stump of Jesse;*
> *a branch will sprout from his roots....*
> *Righteousness will be the belt around his hips,*
> *and faithfulness the belt around his waist.*
> *The wolf will live with the lamb,*
> *and the leopard will lie down with the young goat;*
> *the calf and the young lion will feed together,*
> *and a little child will lead them.*
> *(Isaiah 11:1, 5-6)*

Strengthen the weak hands,
*   and support the unsteady knees.*
Say to those who are panicking:
*   "Be strong! Don't fear!*
*   Here's your God,*
*   coming with vengeance;*
*   with divine retribution*
*   God will come to save you."*
*   (Isaiah 35:3-4)*

Therefore, the Lord will give you a sign. The young woman is pregnant and is about to give birth to a son, and she will name him Immanuel.

*   (Isaiah 7:14)*

If only you would tear open the heavens and come down!
Mountains would quake before you
like fire igniting brushwood or making water boil.
If you would make your name known to your enemies,
the nations would tremble in your presence.
*   (Isaiah 64:1-2)*

Comfort, comfort my people!
*   says your God.*
Speak compassionately to Jerusalem,
*   and proclaim to her that her compulsory service*
*   has ended,*
*   that her penalty has been paid,*
*   that she has received from the* Lord*'s hand double*
*   for all her sins!*

A voice is crying out:
"Clear the Lord*'s way in the desert!*
*   Make a level highway in the wilderness for our God!*

Every valley will be raised up,
    and every mountain and hill will be flattened.
Uneven ground will become level,
    and rough terrain a valley plain.
The LORD's *glory will appear,*
    and all humanity will see it together;
the LORD's *mouth has commanded it."*
                        (Isaiah 40:1-5)

The LORD *God's spirit is upon me,*
    because the LORD *has anointed me.*
He has sent me
    to bring good news to the poor,
    to bind up the brokenhearted,
    to proclaim release for captives,
        and liberation for prisoners,
    to proclaim the year of the LORD's *favor*
        and a day of vindication for our God.
                        (Isaiah 61:1-2a)

These are powerful, familiar passages in which the prophets helped the Israelites envision the coming of a messiah, and, with it, the arrival of comfort, encouragement, and hope. No wonder Paul drew so heavily on Isaiah's words as he wrote to the Romans about the meaning and power of the Incarnation. Throughout the centuries to follow, these words would continue to inspire people, including one of the most famous composers of all time, George Frideric Handel.

HANDEL'S *MESSIAH*

Before the age of thirty, the German-born composer had already achieved superstar celebrity status as one of the most noted composers and conductors in all of Europe. He composed for famous Italian patrons, notable German theaters, and eventually was employed by England's King George I. He was London's most notable and accomplished composer and was considered the most important musical influence in the entire baroque period.

By the time he was fifty-four, his life had turned from superstar celebrity to bankrupt pauper. He was depressed and suffered from physical ailments, including rheumatism. The shine on his star had faded, his fortunes were depleted, and he was looking ahead to spending the rest of his life in debtor's prison. Handel would have been a perfect candidate for an *E! True Hollywood Story*.

And then, two letters arrived. The first was from the duke of Devonshire, who requested that Handel offer his services to, of all things, a benefit concert for charity. Despite his celebrated past, a dejected, desperate Handel took the gig. He was charged with composing a work that would be performed in the Irish capital of Dublin to benefit several jails, Mercer's Hospital on Stephen Street, and the Charitable Infirmary on the Inn's Quay.

The second letter arrived shortly thereafter. It was from an English landowner named Charles Jennens, an eccentric sort of gentleman who had attempted to write lyrics for Handel in the past. But this time was different. Instead of his own words, Jennens sent Handel excerpts from the Old Testament, including many of the passages from Isaiah that you just read.

It was upon reading these texts from Isaiah that inspiration swept through Handel like a flood. In just seven days, he wrote the entire part 1 of his new oratorio. In less than a month, the entire work was complete, and Handel's *Messiah* was born.

It debuted in Dublin in 1742, and it has been debuting in the hearts and minds of countless Advent travelers ever since.

What was it about these Scriptures that transformed and inspired Handel the way they did? Surely, this was not the first time he read them. He had known about Jesus and read these Bible passages countless times. But there was something unique about the way he encountered them this time.

This time, Handel had hit rock bottom. He had acknowledged his desperation and hunger for the salvation and freedom of his very own condition. That's the first thing.

Second, Handel was being asked to give of himself for charity, for the benefit of a community and people in need. He had likely in the past been asked to compose for charity, but this time he was asked while he himself was a person in need. He was like one beggar telling another beggar where to find bread.

The third, and perhaps most significant, factor was this: Handel was compelled by the powerful story of the hope, promise, passion, and triumph of Jesus.

All three of these factors converged in his life to produce a work that would transform the entire musical world and even the world of faith.

Listening to Handel's *Messiah*, coupled with the readings of the Advent prophets, can prompt us to remember these same three things:

1. Acknowledge the depths of our hunger
    and longing.

2. Give of ourselves to others in acts of love
   and peace.
3. Receive the words of Scripture and make
   them our own.

If Scriptures from the Old Testament prophets shaped Paul as he was writing his Letter to the Romans, and if texts like these from Isaiah inspired Handel to write a glorious masterpiece like the *Messiah*, what impact can they make in your life now, as you prepare for a fresh arrival of Jesus this Advent?

UNDERSTANDING THE INCARNATION AS A HISTORICAL EVENT

"His Son was descended from David" (Romans 1:3).

After Paul tells his audience that the good news of God's son was written in the Prophets, he goes on to say that the Son was descended from David.

Few people in the history of Israel are as iconic as David, the shepherd boy who became king and ushered in the height of Israelite power and prestige. In addition to his military accomplishments, David centered the hearts of the people in worship, evidenced by the songs of praise collected in the Psalms. Most important, it was with David that God made a unique covenantal relationship.

And the LORD declares to you that the LORD will make a dynasty for you. When the time comes for you to die and you lie down with your ancestors, I will raise up your

17

REFLECTION QUESTIONS

1. Spend each day over the coming week reading one of these passages from Isaiah on pages 12-14. Consider their original context as words of comfort to God's people in Exile.

2. In what way are you feeling a sense of exile today? How are you longing for "home" in some way?

3. How do these Scriptures from Isaiah give you comfort and encouragement?

4. How do these Scriptures heighten your anticipation for Jesus Christ?

descendant—one of your very own children—to succeed you,
and I will establish his kingdom. He will build a temple for
my name, and I will establish his royal throne forever.

(2 Samuel 7:11b-13)

It is in the context of this covenant with David that Paul understands the second important basis for the incarnation of Jesus. Jesus was not only anticipated by the prophets. He was the fulfillment of God's promise to David. He was descended from David's ancestry, which Matthew highlights in the very first verse in his Gospel—which is the very first verse of the entire New Testament:

A record of the ancestors of Jesus Christ, son of David, son
of Abraham.

(Matthew 1:1)

Now, why is it important to remember that Jesus was born in the line of David? First, it reminds us that God is a God of faithfulness, who always keeps the promises that God has made with us. It is true that during the Babylonian Exile, the Southern Kingdom of Judah lost their line of kings and eventually experienced occupation from one empire to another, including the Romans.

But when it became time for the Messiah to finally arrive and ascend the ultimate throne of God's kingdom forever, it was Jesus, a descendant of David, born to Joseph and Mary.

As much as Advent is a time of hopeful anticipation of God's coming reign, it is also a time of gratitude, acknowledging God's faithfulness in fulfilling the promises that God has made.

But there is another significance to remembering the ancestry of David at the start of Advent. It is a reminder that the Incarnation locates God's revelation in Jesus in an actual moment of human history and has chosen to become part of the human story.

This may feel like a small or insignificant thing. But think about it. The God of the universe, the Creator of all things, the Alpha and Omega of all time, chose to enter human history at a fixed moment in time. Jesus was not a figment of human imagination, and the story of Jesus's life, death, and resurrection is not a myth or a fairy tale. It is an actual historical event, corroborated by real figures of human history who connected to the reality of the historical Jesus.

Think about how the Gospels attest to the historicity of Jesus.

In Luke's Gospel, the passage about the birth of Jesus in chapter 2 begins with these words: "In those days Caesar Augustus declared that everyone throughout the empire should be enrolled in the tax lists. This first enrollment occurred when Quirinius governed Syria" (Luke 2:1-2).

Those are names that we typically skip past in the story, in order to get to more familiar characters like Mary and the shepherds. We don't have a children's Christmas pageant that includes kids dressed like Caesar Augustus or Governor Quirinius. (Could you even imagine?)

Nonetheless, Luke finds it important to name both of these people, in order to locate the incarnation of Jesus in a precise moment in time, corroborated by figures in human history whose existence is attested in non-biblical sources. In other words, Luke wants us to know that Jesus was a real person who entered the world in a real moment in history.

The other well-known political and historical figure in the Gospels, of course, is Pontius Pilate, the governor of the Roman province of Judea. He is named in all four Gospels, most prominently in John. He is also named in the Apostles' Creed, in the section that describes Jesus: "[He] suffered under Pontius Pilate, was crucified, dead, and buried."

Jesus was a real human being, who was born in a particular moment in history, in a specific place in the world.

Now that might seem obvious, and perhaps even inconsequential. But it is important to remember that before Jesus did any miracles or uttered any teachings, and before he died to save our sins and was raised in glory as our Savior, he was born. He was born in a time and place that shaped his view of the world and the people to which he ministered.

After all, isn't that true of you?

Think about the decade when you were born. What was happening in the country, and in the world, that informed the way people at that time defined hope, peace, and prosperity? A person growing up in the United States in the 1940s might have a different way of seeing the world than a person growing up in the 1960s or the first decade of the new millennium.

Think about the place where you grew up. Your neighborhood, town, or city had a unique set of attributes that formed the self-identity of the people living there. Your views of communal spirit, forged out of shared adversity and aspiration, were informed by the particular place you called your hometown.

Think about your religious heritage, if you had one, as you were growing up. Think about how your view of mystery and the divine was shaped by the religious practices and annual observances that were part of your family's faith tradition.

Now, think about how different your life would be if any of these factors surrounding your birth and early childhood were different. If you were born in a different decade, in a different city or even country, into a different religious tradition, how different would your life be right now?

For us to believe in the Incarnation is to believe that Jesus was born into a community, a world, and a time that was saturated with the influences that were unique to that moment.

Jesus was raised in Nazareth, a small town surrounded by hills in lower Galilee, about forty miles north of Bethlehem and fifteen miles from the Sea of Galilee. It was a community of about three hundred Jewish families, most of whom were farmers and livestock herdsmen. Its residents represented enough diversity of skills to make the town self-sufficient, including the carpentry abilities of Jesus's father.

More important, it was an often-overlooked town, far smaller and more isolated than the larger cities throughout Palestine. It had gained such an inferior reputation that early in Jesus's ministry, people disparaged him because of his hometown: "Can anything from Nazareth be good?" (John 1:46).

Jesus was also born into a world of significant political and sociological upheaval. The Jewish community throughout Palestine had long been displaced from any sense of independent self-governance. Even after returning from exile over five hundred years prior, the Jews became vulnerable pawns exchanged from one governing empire to another, from the Persians to the Greeks and Seleucids, and now, to the Romans.

Over that period of a few hundred years, the entire culture of the world had changed. The arrival of Greco-Roman culture introduced the evolution of new styles of cities, roads, and commerce. Greek and Aramaic became the dominant languages, and Greek philosophers gave rise to new ways of thinking and seeing the world.

The Hebrew people would no longer be called Israelites, as they often were throughout the Old Testament, but Jews, a derivative of Judeans, the Southern Kingdom that had returned from exile now living in the land. They had a temple, and they were living in the land of their ancestors, but they had no political king, no true sense of self-governance and independence.

This was the world into which Jesus was born, and the result was that it gave him a unique language to speak (Aramaic) to a people with a unique mindset (longing for liberation) in a unique geopolitical context (Roman occupation). Everything Jesus would say and do was rooted in the time and place into which he entered the world.

His ministry would be based on a message of hope and deliverance from the powers that oppress us, in a language people could understand. In other words, he was born just at the right time for this message to endure, for thousands of years, even until today.

REFLECTION
QUESTIONS

1. How did the community you
    grow up in shape your view of
    the world?

2. How might things be different for
    you today if you were born in a
    different time and place?

3. How does the fact that Jesus
    was born in a specific time and
    place in history give you a deeper
    understanding of his message for
    us today?

CONFESSING THE WRONGS
FROM THE PAST

There is one other way that Paul roots the story of Jesus in the context of the wider human story. It comes from Romans 5, in which Paul reminds people of the origins of sin through the story of Adam and Eve:

Just as through one human being sin came into the world, and death came through sin, so death has come to everyone, since everyone has sinned. Although sin was in the world, since there was no Law, it wasn't taken into account until the Law came. But death ruled from Adam until Moses, even over those who didn't sin in the same way Adam did— Adam was a type of the one who was coming.

(Romans 5:12-14)

We know this story from Genesis well. Adam and Eve were created in the image of God with the capacity of free will, just like all of us. They were instructed to be fruitful and multiply, and to be stewards of creation, just like we are called to do. They were also commanded to refrain from eating from the Tree of the Knowledge of Good and Evil. Yet they were tempted to do so because, according to the serpent, eating from this tree would make them like God.

Unfortunately, that is exactly what they did, and in disobeying God, they not only broke God's commandments, they sinned. According to Paul, sin entered the world—and the human story—through them. The story of what happened in the garden of Eden is true because it typifies the human experience time and again, through our own disobedience and waywardness.

Paul paints a vivid picture for the Romans of how sin operates in our lives. He says it is something that has dominion over us. It holds us hostage. It is like this seemingly inescapable pattern of repetitive behavior and shortcomings that feels impossible to break. That means that in every person, sin is something that keeps us hostage and holds us back from a life of holiness and freedom. Sin is like a recurring pattern, a recording on constant replay, a never-ending loop that cannot be broken.

It is in this context that Paul talks about the significance of Jesus Christ, who was not only foretold by the prophets and was a real person in human history. He was also the "Second Adam," the one through whom new hope was introduced into the world:

> But the free gift of Christ isn't like Adam's failure. If many people died through what one person did wrong, God's grace is multiplied even more for many people with the gift—of the one person Jesus Christ—that comes through grace. . . . So now the righteous requirements necessary for life are met for everyone through the righteous act of one person, just as judgment fell on everyone through the failure of one person. Many people were made righteous through the obedience of one person, just as many people were made sinners through the disobedience of one person. The Law stepped in to amplify the failure, but where sin increased, grace multiplied even more. The result is that grace will rule through God's righteousness, leading to eternal life through Jesus Christ our Lord, just as sin ruled in death.
>
> *(Romans 5:15, 18-21)*

This conviction—that the grace offered through Jesus is the reversal of the sin originating from Adam—is at the heart of Paul's Letter to the Romans. He sees the arrival of Jesus as the dawning of a long-awaited hope that can lead to a new relationship with God. It is based on God's grace—that gift of God that we do not deserve and cannot earn—which we can receive by confessing our sins and professing our faith in Jesus Christ.

In the very next chapter, Paul lays it out clearly:

He died to sin once and for all with his death, but he lives for God with his life. In the same way, you also should consider yourselves dead to sin but alive for God in Christ Jesus.

So then, don't let sin rule your body, so that you do what it wants. Don't offer parts of your body to sin, to be used as weapons to do wrong. Instead, present yourselves to God as people who have been brought back to life from the dead, and offer all the parts of your body to God to be used as weapons to do right. Sin will have no power over you, because you aren't under Law but under grace.

(Romans 6:10-14)

So, here are questions that you may not commonly associate with the Advent season that are central to Paul's Letter to the Romans:

What sins do you need to confess to God?

What is it that you need to repent of in order to make room for a fresh awareness of God's grace and love given to us in Jesus Christ?

A LESSON FROM THE TWELVE STEPS

I have been told by people in the recovery community that the twelve-step program is, in essence, a spiritual process that closely parallels the Christian journey of conversion. It is in Steps 4 through 7 that one confesses one's sins and asks God for forgiveness.

Steps 4 and 5 call us to identify those repeating patterns of thoughts and behaviors that make us stumble and damage our relationships. What are those recurring patterns of sin that you cannot break, no matter how hard you've tried? Like that boulder you simply cannot push to the top? Or like those patterns that are like an endless loop where you are unable to push the button to stop? In the recovery community, we would think of those as addictive behaviors. But for everyone on a spiritual journey, especially at Advent, we should admit that we all have patterns of behaviors that we cannot end on our own, for which we just can't push stop. Steps 4 and 5 invite us to name them.

Then, after conducting a fierce moral inventory and confessing our sins, we are now ready for Steps 6 and 7, forged out of the good news of Jesus Christ who entered the world as the Second Adam. We acknowledge a readiness to have God remove our character defects and ask God to do so.

Prayerfully ponder what are, I believe, the two main words in each of those steps. They both happen to be adverbs. We usually don't pay much attention to adverbs in sentences; they are often filler words. Professional writers would tell us to pay more attention to nouns and verbs for better impact in a sentence.

But here the adverbs are important. *Really, truly* important.

Step 6 includes the word *entirely*. Not partially, not temporarily, but with your whole will and while holding nothing back, ask God to forgive you of your sins. These sins may have seemed so insurmountable that you can't imagine a life that is free from them. You may even want to hold on to that part of your old self, in fear of what you'll discover about yourself in its place. But be ready. Be "entirely" ready to give it all over to God.

Step 7 includes the word *humbly*. Recognize that you cannot put an end to those patterns on your own. Simply say to God, with humility, "I humbly ask you to push stop. I'm tired of listening to that same, repetitive message in my life."

Confession, repentance, and openness to God's forgiveness may seem like an odd invitation during the Advent season. We may more readily associate these activities with Lent and the journey toward the cross. But for Paul and his Letter to the Romans, for the prophets who uttered both words of comfort and challenge to the exiles, and in the name of Jesus who was born in a precise inflection point in history, we are called to surrender ourselves to God.

Entirely and humbly.

A CHRISTMAS LETTER FROM GOD

As we wrap up this first session, ponder again everything we've discovered from Paul's magnificent Letter to the Romans, and what it has taught us about Advent.

Just as Paul interpreted the arrival of Jesus through the expectant words of the prophets, we can look back over our lives

REFLECTION QUESTIONS

1. When was a time when making a confession to God or someone else gave you a sense of freedom and release from your mistakes?

2. In what way do you need Jesus to be your "Second Adam," helping you to overcome some sin in your life?

3. How will you practice confession and repentance at the start of your Advent journey?

and see how God has been working—sometimes unbeknownst to us—toward a deeper appreciation and awareness of God's love for us.

Just as Jesus was born in a real moment in time, in a specific context and community that shaped his actions and his message, we can give thanks for how our own unique background has informed who we are today.

And just as Jesus came to be the "Second Adam" of world history, and to conquer the sins of humanity through his sacrifice, we are called to confess our sins and accept the free gift of grace that God has given to us in Christ.

So, with all those learnings in mind, what might it look like for you to receive a special letter of your own, from the God who created you, loves you, and offers you hope for your journey?

My Child,

I know it's been a long year for you. It has been filled with ups and downs, like most other years. But somehow with every moment of celebration, the heartbreak and anguish you have felt has seemed harsher, more intense, and harder to bear.

I know you know this truth, but I need to reiterate it. It is not my desire for you to suffer. Hardship is not my intent for anyone. Just like it is not my intent for the world to be broken and hurting. That's what sin does. It introduces chaos, it veers the conditions of the world—and even the condition of your life—away from my desires for humanity.

You may not entirely attribute what you've gone through to the sins of the world. But I have seen this from the beginning, since your ancestors made less than ideal choices: sin has consequences, and it hurts.

But here's what I want you to remember. I am more powerful than the brokenness of the world, the hurt in your life, and the sin in the human condition.

That is why I sent my Son, Jesus. Through him, I have overcome the sin in the world. His arrival, his work, his very existence ushered in a new hope for everyone, including and especially for you.

I know that may be hard to understand. After all, he was born two thousand years ago, long before you entered the scene. But even back then, I knew you were coming, just like I am envisioning everyone before you and everyone to come. And because I have such a wide-angle view of eternity, I can assure you of this:

The sin in this world, and the struggles of this life, are nothing compared to the glory to come.

And I'm not just talking about heaven. I mean the steady, sure, and sometimes subtle way I am working to transform you and the rest of this world back to the way I intend things to be.

All of this is possible because of my Son, who entered the world to show you a glimpse of my power, still at work, all these thousands of years later.

Yes, I know life has been hard. Sin is at work, and the suffering is real. But take heart, my child. My grace and forgiveness are greater than sin. And it is here for you.

God

CHAPTER 2

LOVE INCARNATE

The Word of Life Revealed

CHAPTER 2

LOVE
INCARNATE

The Word of Life Revealed

What we have seen and heard, we also announce it to you so that you can have fellowship with us. Our fellowship is with the Father and with his Son, Jesus Christ. We are writing these things so that our joy can be complete.

(1 John 1:3-4)

Years ago, I went on a personal spiritual retreat at a monastery in the midwestern United States. I was feeling adrift in my professional and personal life, and was searching for clarity about some major upcoming decisions.

For most of my time there, I attended prayer services with the monks four times a day. I went on long walks on a forest trail along a large lake. I read and wrote in a spacious study in the lobby of the guest house, with large windows overlooking the beautiful grounds. For three days, I was searching, praying, and discerning some big issues in my life.

The most powerful moments were in spiritual direction sessions with one of the monks, named Father Ambrose. He and I met in a small, sparsely furnished room down the hall from the study. It contained just a table, two comfortable chairs, and the two of us. He began with prayer, asking for God's illumination to be present in our conversation. Then he asked me to share the reason for my visit.

I unpacked everything. It was like opening a spigot to my soul, spilling out all the questions I was pondering about my life and my ministry. I told him about the big decisions I needed to make, weighing for him the pros and cons, the risks and the rewards. I laid it all out as coherently as I could, feeling nervous as I did so, hoping that if I could clearly spell out all the details, he could help me decide what to do.

Father Ambrose listened intently and compassionately, nodding his head, taking it all in. After speaking for what seemed like an eternity, I finally stopped to catch my breath. But I was also waiting with bated breath to see what guidance he would give me.

He sat in silence, his eyes looking upward for a moment as he pondered how to say what was in his heart. Then his eyes locked with mine, and he said, "Magrey, do you believe that God loves you?"

It was my turn to sit in silence. So many thoughts raced into my mind at the moment.

My first thought was, *of course I believe that.* I'm a pastor, after all. As a preacher, my entire career is based on my claiming the conviction that God loves us. If I didn't believe that, then I'm in the wrong business.

My second thought was, *how does this help?* I came here needing answers. I was looking for clarity, for guidance on some big decisions I was needing to make. I didn't need a reminder; I needed direction!

I uttered neither of these thoughts out loud. I simply responded, "Yes, of course."

Father Ambrose then sat in silence, with a kind smile, looking me in the eyes. I began to realize the profound nature of what he was really asking me. He was inviting me to ponder the question at the deepest, most personal level. Not just whether I understood that God loves me. Not just if I claimed that God loves me. He was asking what difference my belief in God's love for me would make in my life at that moment.

Father Ambrose then reminded me that when times are tough, when stressors feel too great to bear, and when decisions seem too difficult to make, we can easily lose sight of the most important truth in our lives.

God loves us.

And it's not just that God loves *us*. God loves *me*. Just like God loves you. God loves you personally, directly, and closely. It's not just *believing* or *understanding* God's love for you. It is experiencing that love in the deepest part of your being. It is recognizing that the very reason for your existence, and the very fiber of your being, is connected to the love that God has for you. Nothing is more important than that. Nothing else matters more than that.

For the duration of my time on that retreat, I continued to ponder Father Ambrose's question, and its implications on the weighty matters I had brought in with me. True, it was not the question I came in asking. But it turned out to be the one I needed most to ask.

By the end of my time, I did receive clarity about many of the things I was wrestling with. And none of it would have emerged had I not remembered the most important truth of all.

No matter what I go through, and no matter how fraught the future may feel, God loves me. That is enough. That is all that matters.

As you move through this Advent season, in what ways do you need to ponder and experience the truth of God's love for you? What burdens and decisions are you carrying that seem insurmountable? Rather than grasp for quick and easy answers, maybe what you are really looking for is a sense of God's deep love for you. And wouldn't it be nice if, somehow, that love from God were so tangible, so real, that your experience of it was unmistakable?

If your answer to those questions is yes, then the letter of 1 John comes to you at just the right time.

1 John, John 1, and Genesis

From the very first verse, we recognize that the epistles of First, Second, and Third John are no ordinary letters. We aren't entirely sure of their authorship, but tradition links the letters with John the apostle, disciple of Jesus, and author of the Gospel of John.

And unlike Paul's epistles, which have a formal greeting structure in which he names his identity and the people to whom he is writing, 1 John gets right to the point with a bold declaration, right out of the gate:

We announce to you what existed from the beginning, what we have heard, what we have seen with our eyes, what we

have seen and our hands handled, about the word of life.
The life was revealed, and we have seen, and we testify and
announce to you the eternal life that was with the Father
and was revealed to us.

(1 John 1:1-2)

John skips the pleasantries and formalities, and begins instead with the bold announcement that God has entered the world in a real, tangible way, in a form that could be seen with their eyes and handled with their hands.

What is that way? It is the "word of life," using a familiar Greek term for the Word "logos."

Now, if that sounds familiar, like we have read that elsewhere in the New Testament, that's because we have. The opening of John's Gospel, which we often read during Advent and Christmas, uses the same term "Logos" and is, in fact, rooted in similar imagery and theology (John 1:1-14).

But here's something even more interesting to think about. John 1 and 1 John are not only similar in literary style and theological themes, they both also parallel the very beginning of the Bible, Genesis 1, in compelling ways.

Let's track the similarities among these three biblical books with a bit of a thought experiment. Imagine each book as a kind of video camera, through which we view God's nature and activity. They each begin with the widest-angle view of the universe, and as we track the four parallels among these three books, we will discover that they narrow their view at each step, ultimately focusing on the same thing: a unique and particular revelation of God to humanity.

Here's what I mean:

Parallel 1: The Widest-Angle View: "In the Beginning"

Genesis 1 opens with a declaration that God existed from the beginning and is the creator of all that is in the universe:

> *When God began to create the heavens and the earth—the earth was without shape or form, it was dark over the deep sea, and God's wind swept over the waters.*
>
> *(Genesis 1:1-2)*

John 1 opens with the Word (*Logos*) that existed from the beginning of time, and who is the universal creator of all that is:

> *In the beginning was the Word*
> *and the Word was with God*
> *and the Word was God.*
> *The Word was with God in the beginning.*
> *Everything came into being through the Word,*
> *and without the Word*
> *nothing came into being.*
>
> *(John 1:1-3)*

First John opens with the bold assertion about the Word (*Logos*) of Life existing from the beginning of time:

> *We announce to you what existed from the beginning, what we have heard, what we have seen with our eyes, what we have seen and our hands handled, about the word of life.*
>
> *(1 John 1:1)*

Parallel 2: Zoom in Closer: God Is Light

Genesis then tells us that the first thing that God created was light, and that God is therefore the source of all light, which defeats the darkness:

God said, "Let there be light." And so light appeared. God
saw how good the light was. God separated the light from the
darkness. God named the light Day and the darkness Night.

There was evening and there was morning: the first day.
(Genesis 1:3-5)

John 1 makes the same move toward the image of light, declaring that the Word who is God is also the source of light for all people:

What came into being t
  hrough the Word was life,
  and the life was the light for all people.
(John 1:3b-4)

First John 1 also paints a vivid picture of the Word as the light of God that has come into the world, through whom we can have fellowship with God.

"God is light and there is no darkness in him at all."…But
if we live in the light in the same way as he is in the light,
we have fellowship with each other, and the blood of Jesus,
his Son, cleanses us from every sin.
(1 John 1:5b, 7)

Parallel 3: Zooming in Even Closer: God Reigns

Genesis moves through the days of creation, each time portraying God as ruling over more and more aspects of the world and its inhabitants:

God said, "Let the waters under the sky come together into
one place so that the dry land can appear." And that's what
happened. God named the dry land Earth, and he named

the gathered waters Seas. God saw how good it was. God said, "Let the earth grow plant life: plants yielding seeds and fruit trees bearing fruit with seeds inside it, each according to its kind throughout the earth."

(Genesis 1:9-11)

The same declaration is found in John 1, that the light that is from God rules over all the darkness of the world and is greater than those who do not recognize the light.

The light shines in the darkness,
and the darkness doesn't extinguish the light.

(John1:5)

The light was in the world,
and the world came into being through the light,
but the world didn't recognize the light.
The light came to his own people,
and his own people didn't welcome him.
But those who did welcome him,
those who believed in his name,
he authorized to become God's children,
born not from blood
nor from human desire or passion,
but born from God.

(John 1:10-13)

Then, in 1 John 2:1-2, we receive the same message, that God is greater than the sin in our lives and the sin in the world:

My little children, I'm writing these things to you so that you don't sin. But if you do sin, we have an advocate with the Father, Jesus Christ the righteous one. He is God's way of dealing with our sins, not only ours but the sins of the whole world.

Parallel 4: The Ultimate Focus: God Enters the Human Story

Then finally, the viewpoint focuses in on the most important truth of all. Genesis tells us that God's very image was expressed in human form when God created the first humans:

> *Then God said, "Let us make humanity in our image to resemble us so that they may take charge of the fish of the sea, the birds in the sky, the livestock, all the earth, and all the crawling things on earth."*
>
> > *God created humanity in God's own image,*
> > *in the divine image God created them,*
> > *male and female God created them.*
> > > *(Genesis 1:26-27)*

In John 1, the ultimate revelation of the Word was in human flesh, in the person of Jesus:

> *The Word became flesh*
> *and made his home among us.*
> *We have seen his glory,*
> *glory like that of a father's only son,*
> *full of grace and truth.*
> > *(John 1:14)*

And 1 John begins its final chapter with the same majestic, poetic assertion, that God became human through the incarnation of Jesus Christ into the world:

This is the one who came by water and blood: Jesus Christ.
Not by water only but by water and blood. And the Spirit is
the one who testifies, because the Spirit is the truth. The three
are testifying—the Spirit, the water, and the blood—and the
three are united in agreement.

(1 John 5:6-8)

These are remarkable parallels among Genesis and both the Gospel and Epistle of John. With each concentric circle, they move through a full and sweeping portrait of the Word of God, first as the Creator of the universe, then as the source of light, then as the ruler over darkness, and finally to the ultimate revelation to humanity in the person of Jesus Christ.

By echoing the themes of Genesis, both John's Gospel and John's Epistle suggest that what happened in the Incarnation was the inauguration of a new creation and a new covenant through a new divine image in human form.

Parallel 1: Jesus is God.
Parallel 2: Jesus is the light.
Parallel 3: Jesus overcomes the darkness of sin.
Parallel 4: Jesus lives and dwells among us.

Together, these ideas from John 1 and 1 John converge to underscore the most important conviction in the Christian faith: God loves you.

The great God and powerful Creator of the universe, who is the source of all light and life, has not only conquered sin and darkness in the world, but has drawn near to you in Jesus. In the incarnation of Jesus, you have the most tangible expression of God's love, made real for you.

When Father Ambrose asked me that question that day on my spiritual retreat, about whether I believed that God loved me, I knew that the best and only response I could have in that moment was to remember Jesus. Jesus came to earth "by water and blood," to be a human just like me. He taught the way of love, so that I could be free of my sins, fears, and griefs. He gave up his life in an act of self-giving love, so that I could be in a full relationship with God. And he rose again so that I could be raised to a new way of loving God and loving all people.

So any time I need a reminder of how much God loves me, I just need to think about the birth, life, death, and resurrection of Jesus. So can you.

INCARNATE WITH ONE ANOTHER

But the letter of 1 John does not just talk about Jesus as the incarnate revelation of God to humans. It goes one step further, to remind us of how God has called each of us to be the conduit of God's love with one another. The incarnation that we anticipate at Advent is not just in the arrival of Jesus in our lives. It is in the expectation that we will take the presence of Jesus and, by "water and blood," become agents of love and healing in our relationships with one another.

This central premise of 1 John is found in this key verse:

> *What we have seen and heard, we also announce it to you so that you can have fellowship with us. Our fellowship is with the Father and with his Son, Jesus Christ. We are writing these things so that our joy can be complete.*
>
> *(1 John 1:3-4)*

REFLECTION QUESTIONS

1. How does thinking about the first chapter of Genesis during Advent strengthen your appreciation of the incarnation of Jesus?

2. In what ways are you experiencing a darkness in your life that can be overcome by the light of Jesus?

3. How would you answer Father Ambrose's question: "Do you believe that God loves you?"

That word *fellowship* is a key word in the New Testament. In Greek, it is *koinonia*, which has a range of translations in English. Most often, it is translated as *fellowship*, as it is in this verse. It can also be translated as *sharing, participation,* and *contribution.* In other words, a community of Christians in fellowship with one another is, in its essence, an active participation, in which people freely give and receive acts of generosity and love with one another.

What is more interesting is that the word *koinonia* has its root in the word *koinos*, which can be translated in two somewhat oppositional ways.

The first is "common," in the sense of "shared," "united," and "holding together." Think about how Christians are to hold things in common such as beliefs, convictions, values, and truths.

All the believers were united and shared everything.
(Acts 2:44)

The community of believers was one in heart and mind. None of them would say, "This is mine!" about any of their possessions, but held everything in common.
(Acts 4:32)

But the second way that *koinos* means "common" is in the sense of "ordinary," "mundane," and even "profane." It is used in verses throughout the New Testament to describe things that Christians are supposed to avoid, things that are defiled and unclean:

They saw some of his disciples eating food with unclean hands. (They were eating without first ritually purifying their hands through washing.)
(Mark 7:2)

> Peter exclaimed, "Absolutely not, Lord! I have never eaten
> anything impure or unclean."
>
> *(Acts 10:14)*

Fascinating. The same word *koinos* can describe both (1) Christian community sharing fully with one another and (2) the kinds of unclean attributes that God's people are taught to avoid. This means that true *koinonia*, fellowship with one another in Christ, is one where followers of Jesus both bring out the best in one another to be more loving, and help one another avoid that which is sinful and unholy.

That is why 1 John is filled with practical guidance on how to love one another, so that everyone can grow in their love of God and others.

FELLOWSHIP IN TRUTH AND LOVE

So since we have received the ultimate revelation of God's love in the incarnation of Jesus, and if our task is to embody that love in our relationships with one another, how do we make that happen? What does full fellowship with one another look like?

Taken together, the Gospel of John and the Letter of 1 John identify two key qualities that should guide our relationships with God and one another: truth and love. To put it most simply, John's Gospel is about truth, and John's epistles are about love. John's Gospel is about believing and being clear about who Jesus is. (John's Gospel contains the words *truth* and *belief* far more than any other book in the Bible.) And John's epistles are primarily about love, and living fully in the way of Jesus.

So in order to have full *koinonia* with one another, in which we prompt one another toward more loving participation and help one another refrain from actions that are sinful and unhealthy, here is the question we can ask: how can we live in ways that are both truthful and loving with one another?

Think about the importance of holding truth and love in balance with one another, especially in the kinds of hard decisions and difficult conversations that you have had with other people. Discussions that have an imbalance between truth and love can be at best unhealthy, and at worst, harmful.

Speaking truth without love can lead to condescension, name-calling, and entrenched tribalism. But love without truth can lead to a drift in basic morals and values, a loss of ideals, and a failure to move forward as a society.

Author Warren Wiersbe once said, "Truth without love is brutality and love without truth is hypocrisy."[1]

We need both truth and love in the way we talk to one another, debate important issues, and have *koinonia* with one another.

Consider a strained relationship you have had at some point in your life with someone you love. In order for any loving relationship to work, whether it be in a marriage or a family relationship or a close friendship, there needs to be a balance between speaking and hearing truth, and doing so with love. In a relationship, sometimes the most loving thing you can do is to speak truth to someone, along with being open to hearing hard truths about yourself. And sometimes, the most truthful thing to do is to love that person, even when it's hard.

Author Timothy Keller, in his book on marriage, put it this way: "Love without truth is sentimentality; it supports and affirms us but keeps us in denial about our flaws. Truth without love is harshness; it gives us information but in such a way that we cannot really hear it."[2]

For Christian people, truth and love are two sides of the same coin. Especially for Methodists like me and others in the Wesleyan tradition.

I once heard a lecture by my friend Dr. Paul Chilcote, a longtime professor of Wesleyan studies. He shared the story of John Wesley's two conversion experiences.

The first one is well known. We call it his "Aldersgate experience." Wesley was struggling in his faith about how to know, how to believe, that he was truly saved. One night, on May 24, 1738, he stumbled upon a small group gathering in a room on Aldersgate Street. The group was studying the Bible together, and the leader was reading from Martin Luther's preface to the Book of Romans, about how God has done everything necessary for us to be saved, and our salvation required no merit or works on our part. Wesley would write what happened next: "While [the leader] was describing the change which God works in the heart through faith in Christ, I felt my heart strangely warmed. I felt I did trust in Christ, Christ alone, for salvation; and an assurance was given me that He had taken away *my* sins, even *mine*, and saved *me* from the law of sin and death."[3]

That was Wesley's first conversion experience, according to Dr. Chilcote, in which John Wesley developed a "passion for the truth."

But there would be a second conversion experience for Wesley. He would take the truth of the gospel and preach it near and far, out in the countryside and in the city. And as he traveled throughout England, his eyes were opened to the physical needs of the people around him. The poor, those living on the streets, the sick lacking adequate health care, the illiterate in need of proper schooling, the hungry in need of food. And as a result, John Wesley became convicted to address the real-life needs of people, and make that a part of his mission.

This was Wesley's second conversion experience, according to Dr. Chilcote. From that moment on, Wesley not only had a "passion for the truth," he had a "compassion for people."

I've never forgotten that statement.

That is how to live both the Gospel of John and the epistles of John. In every aspect of our lives, in our relationships with others and in the character of our society, we need to develop a passion for truth and a compassion for people.

So, as we march toward Christmas Eve, let's explore a few practical ways that you might live with both truth and love, by seeing how John's epistle teaches us both.

First, let's look at truth through the lens of 1 John.

LIVING TRUTHFULLY, LIKE JESUS

Some of you may remember the classic game show *To Tell the Truth*, which debuted in the 1950s and has had updated versions through today. The premise of the show was that a panel of celebrities interrogated three ordinary-looking guests, all of whom claimed to be the same person. At the end of the questioning, the celebrities would each choose which of the three they believed was telling the truth.

And then the host Bud Collyer would say, "Will the real person please stand up?"

The show later spawned imitation programs such as *What's My Line?*, *I've Got a Secret,* and *The Moment of Truth.* (It seems we've always had a fascination with the art of telling a lie.)

And, to tell you the truth, so does the First Epistle of John. John has a fibbing fixation. The word *liar* is one of his favorite words, and he uses it as many times in his five brief chapters as in all the other New Testament books combined. His letter reads like one long polygraph test.

In chapter 1: You know you are a liar if you say that you are sinless. (1:8-10)

In chapter 2: You know you are a liar if say you believe in God but refuse to keep God's commandments (2:4).

In chapter 2: You know you are a liar if you deny that Jesus is the Messiah (2:22).

In chapter 4: You know you are a liar if you say you love God but hate another person (4:20).

And in chapter 5: You know you are a liar if you say you believe in God but do not believe that Jesus is whom the church says he is (5:10).

Those are harsh words! No other book in the Bible puts things quite this bluntly, and at the end you almost expect John to say that your pants are on fire! At the very least, we might hear John ask, "Will the real follower of Jesus please stand up?"

Well, if you want to know who the real followers of Jesus are, John tells us how to spot them, in chapter 2, verses 5 and 6: He says, "But the love of God is truly perfected in whoever keeps his word. This is how we know we are in him. The one who claims to remain in him ought to live in the same way as he lived."

In other words, it's not simply about saying whether you are a Christian. It's about following Jesus, living as Jesus lived, and thinking as he thought.

Several years ago, the research organization Barna Group conducted an interesting survey among self-professing Christians. They wanted to determine whether Christians acted more like Jesus or more like Pharisees.[4]

Their premise was straightforward. They defined following Jesus to mean modeling both his actions and his attitudes. To be more like a Pharisee would mean the same thing: model the actions and the attitudes of the Pharisees. The survey was only twenty questions long, with five questions covering each of the following categories: (1) Actions of Jesus, (2) Attitudes of Jesus, (3) Actions of a Pharisee, and (4) Attitudes of a Pharisee.

Each question was based on insights from the Gospels themselves. The surveyors asked questions based on the actions and attitudes of Jesus and the Pharisees recounted in the Gospels—things like feeling compassion for those who aren't following God or seeing God working in people's lives even when they aren't following God (attitudes of Jesus), or pointing out those who don't have the right doctrine or theology (actions of a Pharisee).

The questions were hard to answer honestly. Yet in the spirit of 1 John, it's important that we face our inner lives honestly—that we tell the truth about ourselves even if it means confronting some hard realities.

Barna shared the results of their survey, and it turns out that a majority of Christians actually live more like Pharisees than Jesus.

Fifty-one percent of people who say they follow Jesus are actually more self-righteous in their actions and attitudes.

And what percentage of people are truly more like Jesus in their minds and behaviors? Fourteen percent. Only one in seven.

Wow.

Again, 1 John 2:4 puts it this way: "The one who claims, 'I know him,' while not keeping his commandments, is a liar, and the truth is not in this person."

Are you more Christlike in attitudes, but not action? More Christlike in action, but not in your attitude toward others? Or are you both? Or are you neither?

I don't know about you, but my own reflections on these questions show that I have a long way to go in going ten-for-ten on the Jesus questions, and zero-for-ten on the Pharisee questions. I suspect that's true for you, too. There is comfort in knowing that you and I aren't alone. It's not only a problem for Christians today; it has been this way since the first century. It's why John wrote this whole letter to begin with.

But the stakes are high. Survey results like these underscore why many people outside the church view Christians the way they do. Too many unchurched or formerly churched people have long thought that Christians are less like the Jesus they claim to follow, in actions and in attitudes.

May we each live in a way that is much less like the 51 percent in the Barna survey, and more like the 14 percent.

More like Jesus, less like the Pharisees.

In the 1950s, there was a man named Clinton H. Goodwin, who lived in Los Angeles. At the age of twenty, Goodwin descended into a life of crime. He burglarized several stores and gas stations, was involved in a gunfight, and was eventually arrested, tried, and sentenced to San Quentin prison. He had made a mess of his life.

While in prison, he was introduced to Jesus Christ by one of the chaplains. He turned his life over to Christ, and when he was released, he determined to devote his life to following Jesus, both in action and in attitude. He became the superintendent of the Union Rescue Mission, the largest relief and support organization in Los Angeles that served thousands of unhoused persons throughout the city.

In 1958, he appeared on that very television game show, *To Tell the Truth*. Along with him was a retired army officer and a public relations attorney. But there was only one Clinton Goodwin, only one former burglar turned minister, the only one of the three who was telling the truth.

Among the celebrity questioners was a young, fresh celebrity named Betty White and a young newsman named Mike Wallace. Neither of them guessed who the real Clinton Goodwin was.

But two of the panelists did. They guessed it right, and they said it was because, "there was something different about the real Clinton Goodwin." One of them said "there was a sort of kindness and gentleness" about him that made them believe that he not only did the right things, but he had the right attitude too.

How about you? If you were in a lineup of people who all claimed to be followers of Jesus, would people know that it was you? And would you be telling the truth?

First John 2:6 says: "The one who claims to remain in him ought to live in the same way as he lived."

Would people say you were more like a Jesus follower or a Pharisee? Most important, what would happen if Jesus were to say, "Would the real follower of mine please stand up?"

And would you be telling the truth?

LIVING LOVINGLY, LIKE JESUS

Having explored what it means to live in truth with one another, we turn to the second pillar of Christian fellowship in 1 John. Its call to love is a central premise of the letter, and is an important part of our Advent journey.

What does it mean to love one another, in light of God's love revealed in Jesus?

There are many words in the English language that are both nouns and verbs. Words like *challenge* and *color*, *question* and *rhyme*. Same word, describing both things and actions.

Some of these words were originally nouns in their primitive root form and developed later into verbs. These are called denominal verbs. Words like *dust*, *summer*, and *bicycle* are all verbs that started as nouns.

But then there are words that were originally verbs that became nouns. And in the Greek language, the language of the

REFLECTION QUESTIONS

1. Why do you think truthfulness is an important aspect of our relationships with one another?

2. Why do you think 1 John connects truthfulness with following God's commandments?

3. Where do you find yourself among the results and conclusions of the Barna survey?

New Testament, the language of 1 John, this is the case for the word *love*. The word for love is *agapao*, which is, in its primitive origin, a verb. It is later derived as a noun throughout the rest of the New Testament.

So, at its core, love is an action.

When Jesus said, "Love your neighbor as yourself," (Mark 12:31) he was quoting the Old Testament Book of Leviticus. He pulled out those five words as a summary of a larger set of actions that defined what loving others means, in Leviticus 19. It's a section of thirteen verses that talk about feeding the poor and caring for strangers. Not stealing or lying. Treating others fairly and not holding a grudge. Honoring the elderly, and caring for the immigrant as if they were your family.

And tucked in the midst of all those actions in Leviticus 19 are those five words: "Love your neighbor as yourself" (v. 18).

Love is not just something we fall into, or create, or feel for someone else. It is not just a goal or an ideal. It is more than simply a core quality of Christian character.

Love is something we do. It is a deliberate choice, to orient our hearts and minds in a certain way toward other people. It does not come naturally. Other base instincts would want us to treat others in ways that create distance and separation from one another. Love takes effort. It involves risk. It can result in disappointment, and sometimes even grief.

In other words, to love means to grow.

Dr. David Gushee quotes the great Reinhold Niebuhr in his book *Introducing Christian Ethics*. He writes:

> Niebuhr suggests that love is always beckoning
> us to transcendent heights which we can never

quite reach, but to which we must continually aspire. Love constantly calls us to greater purity in our motivations and greater breadth of application in practice. We must love—not just a little but more—then more—then more. We must love—not just self, but partner, not just partner but children, not just children but neighbors, and on and on. We must love—with more intelligence, more effectiveness, more care, more self-giving. If we think we have arrived at love, we know nothing about it.[5]

Love is first a verb before it is a noun. So, love involves movement, growth, and change.

And it makes sense for love to involve change, right? Because after all, love involves relationships, and relationships change over time. Every relationship does. Whether it's your relationship with your partner, or your children, or your parents. Whether it's with your coworkers, your community, or even God, the nature of your relationship changes, so you must adapt the ways you express and share love in that relationship.

I love the way Dr. Gushee describes how the love between parents and children changes over time:

As for the relationship between parents and children, it goes through stages. When our children are little, we sacrifice greatly, there is little mutuality, and there is more than occasional rescuing required. As the children grow, the mutuality between parent and child grows in lovely ways, though there is always the possibility of arduous sacrifice or occasional

urgent effort to deliver from disaster. When we
get old, the balance shifts, and we may be the
ones who need our grown children to sacrifice
for us or even to rescue us.[6]

Relationships change. So, the way we love in those relationships must also change.

In fact, here is another word that is both a noun and verb. It's the word *time*. And in some ways, love and time are deeply connected.

Loving others takes time.

The way we learn to love one another changes over time.

Sometimes, we can't fully appreciate how others have loved us until time has passed, and we see it in retrospect.

And here's something else we all know about time: each of us has a limited amount of it in our lifetimes.

As we age, time becomes more of a pressure than a privilege. We push ourselves to accomplish more and there never seems to be enough time in a day. We hit a point in our lives—some people call it midlife—when we realize that there is more time behind us than before us. And as much as we plan and order our lives, we realize that time feels like it is slipping through our fingers.

As time marches on, we feel more restless.

And that's when we most need to remember that the greatest use of our time is spending it with love.

One of the greatest privileges I have as a pastor is to be alongside families in the immediate wake of a loved one's death. As we plan the funeral service together, I listen for stories and memories they share with me.

And every time, there is a common denominator among all those stories, among all the different families that I have ministered to over the years. People aren't best remembered by their possessions or their achievements. They aren't celebrated for their toys or trophies.

What a family remembers most are the relationships. What they remember most is that person's love throughout their time with them.

We all have a limited amount of time, but the love we share can make an unlimited impact.

LIVING IN TRUTH AND LOVE

Having explored each of the two pillars of truth and love in 1 John, we can pull it all together to discover how the revelation of God in Jesus can bring us to closer fellowship with one another. How can truth and love strengthen our relationships with one another?

Here are three practical statements of guidance from 1 John.

First, show more than speak. First John 3:18 says, "Little children, let's not love with words or speech but with action and truth." For John, demonstrating love is more truthful than merely speaking love. Speaking love is important, but practicing love involves more self-sacrifice, and more risk-taking. It was Mark Twain who added a quip to a familiar saying when he said, "Actions speak louder than words but not nearly as often." Someone else put it this way: "Actions speak louder than words, but consistency speaks louder than both." Demonstrating love for others with consistency is more truthful than mere words.

Second, stay connected. Even when your relationship with someone is strained, or even when a large segment of the country seems to have a completely different ideological perspective than you do, do your best to stay connected in some way. Because in matters of both love and truth, connection is better than isolation. Just as you need two people to experience love, you need two people to experience truth. Just as love only happens in a mutual relationship of giving and receiving, you cannot corner the market on truth on your own. We are reliant on the perspectives and insights of other people to come to a fuller sense of truth together. And all of us need to be in a relationship with God. First John 3:20 says, "Even if our hearts condemn us, God is greater than our hearts and knows all things." A balance between truth and love means staying connected to one another and to God.

And finally, hold your truth lovingly. This means recognizing that there are multiple stories and different perspectives in any given situation, not just your own. Work to see the situation through the story of the other person, recognize their humanity, and see the image of God in them. First John 4:19-21 contains these powerful words:

> *We love because God first loved us. Those who say, "I love God" and hate their brothers or sisters are liars. After all, those who don't love their brothers or sisters whom they have seen can hardly love God whom they have not seen! This commandment we have from him: Those who claim to love God ought to love their brother and sister also.*

Hold your truth lovingly. Lean into the discomfort, and find the humanity in one another.

First John contains beautiful, rich insights into the very question that Father Ambrose asked me during my spiritual retreat. "Do you believe that God loves you?" First John would first point to the incarnation of Jesus as the most vivid expression of God's love. His arrival in the world was the culmination of a story that began "in the beginning," according to both Genesis and John's Gospel. In Jesus is the source of light that vanquishes the darkness and despair of the human experience, including all that I was carrying into that retreat. By focusing on Jesus, I could strengthen my belief in God's love for me.

But there was a dimension to Father Ambrose's question that was just as important as believing in God's love for me. It reminded me that I could find God's love in my relationships with others. It was in the community, the fellowship, the *koinonia* of other Christians that I could see the incarnate presence of God's love for me.

When I returned to Florida, I spent some intentional time with trusted friends, colleagues, and loved ones, who came alongside me in my ongoing spiritual journey. Over time, and even until today, I can affirm with greater conviction that yes, indeed, I believe in God's love for me.

With Christmas right around the corner, we will soon be celebrating the greatest example of truth and love made real to us. For in Jesus, God decided to show us love, not just speak it. God decided to connect with us, not just leave us on our own. And God has shown us how to strengthen our fellowship with one another, lovingly and truthfully.

A CHRISTMAS LETTER FROM GOD

As we wrap up this second session, ponder again everything we've discovered from John's first epistle.

The letter connects us to the One who was at "the very beginning"—the Creator who spoke all things into being (Genesis), the Savior who came to us as a light for all people (Gospel of John), and the Spirit who is rekindling our relationships with one another in truth and love (1 John).

While it is our tendency to fixate on the problems we are facing in any given moment, we can take comfort that God has been guiding us and all humanity long before we encountered our present-day problems.

Because of Jesus, we can have renewed fellowship with one another, especially those with whom we disagree and from whom we are different. We are called to be both truthful and loving with one another.

Most of all, the incarnation of Jesus reminds us of the most important idea of all: we are loved. God loves us fully, despite our shortcomings, and deeply, despite our doubts and disbelief. God's love for you is not contingent on your ability to earn it, understand it, or claim it.

As a clergy friend of mine loves to say to his congregation, "God loves you. Period."

So with these lessons in mind, what might it look like for you to receive a special letter of your own, from the God who created you, loves you, and strengthens you for your journey?

My Child,

Take a moment today, in the midst of your busyness and stress, to acknowledge what an adventure life is. No single day is the same. What you have experienced in the past is over, and you cannot predict what will happen tomorrow. All you know is the moment at hand.

So know this: I am with you in this moment, and I love you.

I have been with you since the very beginning, just as I was there at the start of creation itself. I spoke light into being, formed the stars and fashioned the planets, nurtured life into its gradual and glorious development, and gave humanity my very own image when it took its first breath.

But there is one more thing that I created that I want you to remember. I created love. I created relationships and relationality. I created longing and trust, interdependence and support. I created the capacity for people to love one another, because that is a part of myself, my image, my ability to love without condition.

So with all that you are going through today, remember love. Remember that I love you, and that you can love those around you.

I know it's not easy to love. Humanity is diverse and varied, the way I intended it. But it is also wayward and sinful, in a way I did not. That's why I came to you in Jesus, to show you the depth of my love for you and the way you can love one another.

Truthfully. Lovingly. Fully. That's the way I intend it.

And one more thing. Not only have I been in your past. I am in your future. I will never stop loving you and humanity into redemption. No matter how hard things get in your relationships with others, no matter how hopeless things seem in the world, don't give up. I am, and always will be, working toward a better future. You can join me in that, one step at a time.

My love will never end.

God

REFLECTION QUESTIONS

1. How will your belief in God's love for you change your perspective and behavior for the better?

2. What, in your experience, is the relationship between love and time?

3. How will you practice the concepts of showing versus telling, staying connected, and holding your truth lovingly?

CHAPTER 3

FULLY HUMAN

Joy in Humility

CHAPTER 3

FULLY HUMAN

Joy in Humility

Therefore, if there is any encouragement in Christ, any comfort in love, any sharing in the Spirit, any sympathy, complete my joy by thinking the same way, having the same love, being united, and agreeing with each other. Don't do anything for selfish purposes, but with humility think of others as better than yourselves. Instead of each person watching out for their own good, watch out for what is better for others. Adopt the attitude that was in Christ Jesus:

> *Though he was in the form of God,*
> > *he did not consider being equal with God something to exploit.*
> *But he emptied himself*
> > *by taking the form of a slave*
> > *and by becoming like human beings.*
> *When he found himself in the form of a human,*
> > *he humbled himself by becoming obedient to the point of death,*
> > *even death on a cross.*
> *Therefore, God highly honored him*

and gave him a name above all names,
so that at the name of Jesus everyone
in heaven, on earth, and under the earth might bow
and every tongue confess
that Jesus Christ is Lord, to the glory of
God the Father.

(Philippians 2:1-11)

In every major scene in the story of Jesus's birth, there is an interaction between the human and the divine. Think about it. Every time we are introduced to a new character in the birth narratives, it is in the context of some divine visitation of an unsuspecting human being.

In Luke, the first people we meet are Elizabeth and Zechariah, an aging, childless couple. Then one day, an angel visits Zechariah in the Temple, and soon after there is a pregnancy that would usher John the Baptist into the world.

When we first meet Mary, she is a young girl suddenly visited by the angel Gabriel, who calls on her to carry the child who would be the Messiah. Later in Luke, the shepherds are out in the fields, guarding their sheep, when an angel appears in the night sky, followed by a choir of angels, heralding good news of great joy.

In Matthew, the first person we meet is Joseph, who is visited by an angel through a dream. Through the angel, God summons of him the courage to keep his relationship with Mary, despite pressure to dismiss her. And even after the birth of Jesus, when we meet the magi, these foreign astrologers encounter a sign in the heavens that impels them to visit the Holy Family.

At every turn, we see the same theme. There are human beings—unsuspecting, doubtful, fearful, and worried. They are met by the divine—through an angel, a dream, a star. Then their lives are changed forever.

And what is the common denominator among all these people, all these interactions? They all point to Jesus, who is the not just the pivotal character for each of these people, but the bridge between the human and the divine for all the world, for all eternity.

Here is what we know about ourselves as humans, and about our sinful condition: we cannot save ourselves. We need someone who is *more than* human to become human in order to meet us where we are and to help us become all that God has called us to be.

In short, we need Jesus, who is the bridge between heaven and earth, who, though being God, became human, just like us.

THE LAND OF MISFIT TOYS

We all have our favorite Christmas movies and television shows. Among my most cherished childhood traditions was watching *Rudolph the Red-Nosed Reindeer*, a show many of us know well.

If you've seen it, you know the story. Rudolph goes on a trip with two traveling companions: Hermey the Elf, who wanted to be a dentist, and the wild-eyed explorer Yukon Cornelius. But the part that always enchanted me was when they found themselves in a place called The Island of Misfit Toys.

It was a land filled with poor, rejected toys that no one wanted because there was something wrong with them. There was a toy train with square wheels, a water pistol that squirted jelly, a doll with low self-esteem, an elephant covered with spots. All of them banished to exile, shunned to the fringe of humanity, never to be chosen or loved.

I suspect this scene was in the show to teach children about empathy and compassion. It would teach us not to judge others for their shortcomings, because, in fact, all of us have them.

And boy, did it work. I didn't know this until recently, but when the show first debuted in 1964, the original version ended with the toys left on that island, never being rescued.

That elicited hundreds of angry letters from children after the show premiered. Children were so upset that the toys were left there, forgotten. So the following year, the producers changed the script. They added a scene, a correction that became a new part of the show in 1965 and has been there ever since, in which the misfit toys find homes.

At the end of the show, Rudolph and Santa descend onto the island. Santa scoops up the misfit toys, puts them into his bag, and loads them onto his sleigh, giving them to boys and girls around the world who eagerly receive them and give them the one thing they have always wanted and never had: the gift of love and acceptance.

Let's just face it. This Advent season, and all year round, we are all just a bunch of misfit toys.

Oh, I know, we don't want to admit it. We spend a lot of time and effort trying to project to other people that things are a lot better than they actually are. But you and I well know deep down inside that we have our own hang-ups, habits, and heartaches. We live in relationships that are broken, a past that is full of shame and guilt, and a future that is fraught with worry. We have the constant replay of old tapes in our minds that would convince us that we are far removed from the kind of life we know we should live.

If only someone could come and rewrite the script for us. To add a scene. To do for us what we cannot do for ourselves: to come down to earth, join us at our level, maybe even become a misfit toy too, and show us what unconditional love and second chances might look like.

That, in a nutshell, is what the incarnation of Jesus is all about.

And of all the epistles in the New Testament, it is Paul's Letter to the Philippians that captures the self-emptying, self-giving love of Jesus most beautifully and most powerfully.

PHILIPPIANS: THE EPISTLE OF JOY

There are many reasons that Philippians stands out among the other books of the New Testament. Unlike the other epistles, it is not written to address some problem or conflict that is dividing an entire faith community. It is the most joyful of all Paul's letters, a theme that we will emphasize later in this chapter. The third week of Advent is typically devoted to the theme of joy, so it's fitting to explore the Letter to the Philippians here.

But the most distinguishing feature of Philippians is in its second chapter, which contains what is widely regarded as one of the first Christian hymns. It is the clearest, most comprehensive explanation for the incarnation of Jesus.

> *Though he was in the form of God,*
>> *he did not consider being equal with God something to exploit.*
>
> *But he emptied himself*
>> *by taking the form of a slave*
>> *and by becoming like human beings.*
>
> *When he found himself in the form of a human,*
>> *he humbled himself by becoming obedient to the point of death,*
>> *even death on a cross.*
>
> *Therefore, God highly honored him*
>> *and gave him a name above all names,*
>
> *so that at the name of Jesus everyone*
>> *in heaven, on earth, and under the earth might bow*
>> *and every tongue confess*
>>> *that Jesus Christ is Lord, to the glory of God the Father.*
>
> *(Philippians 2:6-11)*

Here's what is remarkable about this hymn from Philippians. It offers a direct contradiction to the ways of the world. Rather than suggesting that the way to greatness is a steady climb upward, with more power, fame, and possessions, this hymn declares the exact opposite. The way of Jesus is the path of downward mobility, the way of servanthood, an inverse bell curve to the ways of the world.

Jesus, who is equal to God, came down to earth, to become human. The one who existed at the very beginning, who spoke light into existence and brought the universe into being, elected to become the very same substance as earth. The Creator became the creature. The God of infinite power became the same collection of oxygen, nitrogen, and carbon as you and me. God chose to breathe the same air and walk the same ground as us. The divine became human, to be a bridge between both.

And why? This may be the most intriguing point that Paul makes to the Philippians.

THOUGH VS. BECAUSE

The first word in the hymn is often translated as "Though." Though Jesus was God, he did not consider being God as something to be exploited. When we hear that sentence, leading with the word *though*, we may conclude that Jesus considered his equality with God as something to negate, ignore, or suppress in order to be become human. The word *though* suggests that Jesus had to settle some inherent contradiction within himself in order to come to earth.

But here's what's interesting: that word *though*, in the Greek, can also be translated as *because*.

Doesn't that completely change the way we would interpret this verse?

Because Jesus was God, he did not consider being God as something to be exploited.

It means there is no contradiction between being God and being self-giving. It suggests that it is within God's very nature to be gracious and generous. The work of Jesus is not God concealed, but God revealed.

What follows after this opening sentence is nothing less than the entire salvation story, and the entire Christian liturgical year, summarized in a few short verses.

- *Jesus was equal to God, who existed from the very beginning.* (Genesis 1:1)
- *He emptied himself... by becoming like human beings.* (Philippians 2:7; Advent, the Incarnation)
- *He humbled himself by becoming obedient to the point of death, even death on a cross.* (Philippians 2:8; Lent, the Crucifixion)
- *Therefore, God highly honored him and gave him a name above all names.* (Philippians 2:9; Easter, the Resurrection)
- *So that at the name of Jesus everyone... might bow and every tongue confess that Jesus Christ is Lord.* (Philippians 2:10; Pentecost, the Church, Christ the King)

There it is. An inverse bell curve. Jesus existed from the very beginning, became human and died, and was raised to glory to save all humanity.

And all of this happened, not despite Jesus being God, but because Jesus was God.

So just imagine. There was baby Jesus, entering this world through a very human birth, opening his eyes for the first time. Because he was human, he experienced all the wonder of the world rushing in for the first time through his physical senses. He felt the touch of his mother's hand, heard the words of his father's voice, and he opened his eyes to those around him.

And because he was also fully God, it must have been amazing to see in these people the very reason he came to earth to begin with.

Perhaps when he first looked at his mother, Mary, he saw in her the face of a beloved misfit. In her eyes was the soul of a weary traveler, who traversed not just ninety miles of hot, dusty road on the way to Bethlehem, but the long weary road of nine months of public scorn and scrutiny, day after day dealing with townsfolk who stigmatized and marginalized her.

Perhaps when he saw his father, Joseph, he saw in him the face of a beloved misfit too. In his eyes was the fatigue of a man who had been ridiculed for being weak and unprincipled, for refusing to do the expected thing and cast Mary aside. It had to be hard to be the laughingstock of the town.

And perhaps when Jesus saw the shepherds, he saw another group sleeping in the fields, raising livestock, getting dirty, doing hard work that few others likely wanted to do and yet, in the process, doing the work that Moses and David had done centuries earlier.

In other words, when Jesus first opened his eyes, I'll bet he saw a Nativity of Misfit Toys.

But there's more. I'd like to think that when he first opened his eyes, he also saw you and me, as he saw the fullness of humanity. He saw your condition, and he saw mine. He saw through your facade. He saw the battles you lose every day against your sins and weaknesses. He saw the pain of your broken relationships. He saw your separation from God, your deep-down doubts, and the way that you feel lost in your life. He saw your longing for acceptance, and he saw your misery in a world that seems so twisted and full of suffering.

And that is exactly why he came. Because in the original script, in the way it had always been since Adam and Eve, we were left all alone and miserable. But God wouldn't have it that way.

So, Jesus came to this island of misfit toys and showed us love by becoming a misfit himself. Not despite being God, but because he was God.

EMPATHY, CURIOSITY, HUMILITY

Philippians 2 teaches us a lot about the Incarnation, giving us the most poetic and precise language about why and how Jesus came to earth as a human being. But it's important to remember the words that introduce the Christ hymn, the prologue to this ancient poem, that give us important guidance for holy living.

> *Therefore, if there is any encouragement in Christ, any comfort in love, any sharing in the Spirit, any sympathy, complete my joy by thinking the same way, having the same love, being united, and agreeing with each other. Don't do anything for selfish purposes, but with humility think of others as better than yourselves. Instead of each person watching out for their own good, watch out for what is better for others. Adopt the attitude that was in Christ Jesus.*
>
> *(Philippians 2:1-5)*

Reading these verses might make us wonder what was happening in the Philippian church that would prompt Paul to write these words to them. They appear to be instructions, even admonishment, for some unnamed conflict within the community there. While there is no overt disagreement

REFLECTION QUESTIONS

1. In what ways do you feel like a "misfit toy"? How do others you know feel like they are "misfit toys"?

2. How does the second chapter of Philippians bring you comfort and encouragement?

3. How do you think the incarnation of Jesus gives you hope for your situation?

plaguing them like in other churches to which Paul was writing, it turns out even the Philippians were not immune to the kind of me-first mindset that is a basic part of human nature.

That includes the kinds of relationships, communities, and even churches that you and I are a part of.

After all, there are many ways that you and I might define ourselves, and how we might identify with certain demographics, subcultures, and communities. We live in a world where people are commonly categorized along the lines of race, gender, religion, socioeconomic status, and many others.

But a few years ago, one study suggested that when it comes to choosing who we connect with the most, and how we relate to other people, the one filter we choose most commonly, the one identity we hold most closely, is our political affiliation.

That was the conclusion of Stanford professor Shanto Iyengar and others, who in 2017 published their findings in the *European Journal of Political Research*.[1] They discovered that people define themselves by their political perspective more closely than their race, cultural heritage, or even their religion. Iyengar and his co-authors said this is not only true for Americans, but for other well-established democracies as well.

I doubt this comes as much of a surprise to you. As you read this, you may have gone through another Thanksgiving holiday, and may be going through another Christmas season, when the biggest concern for many people—perhaps including yourself—was the hope that your family could remain civil when partisan topics came up over the holiday dinner table.

You may experience that type of filter at work when you find out where someone gets their news from or hear their thoughts on major issues of the day or listen to them describe the general state of the country and world. And how quickly are we both ready and eager to put someone into those boxes of conservative, moderate, or liberal, as soon as we can "get a handle on them"?

No, this is not much of a surprise, even for people in the church.

Will Willimon, the former dean of Duke Chapel and retired bishop of The United Methodist Church, told a story of the very first church that he ever served when he was just a young pastor.

Willimon drove out on a Saturday to meet the lay leader and see the church for the first time, but arrived before the church member did. He walked up to front door of the church and saw a large chain and padlock barring the door shut.

When the lay leader arrived, Willimon said, "Glad you are here to open the lock on the door."

To which the church member said, "Oh, that ain't our lock. The sheriff put that there. Things got rough here at the meeting last month. Folks started yelling at one another, carting off furniture they had given to the church. So, I called the sheriff and he came out here and put that lock on the door until the new preacher could get here and settle 'em down."

The name of that church? Friendship Methodist Church. A misnomer, if there ever was one.[2]

Well, with this curse of division and disunity that plagues our communities today, we can begin to see why the ancient hymn in Philippians 2 needed to be preceded by Paul's introductory words. No, Paul doesn't address with specificity the exact issues dividing the Christians in Philippi, like he does in letters to the other churches. But he does plead with the Philippians—and with each of us—to "[think] the same way, having the same love, being united, and agreeing with each other" (v. 2).

This, Paul said, would "complete my joy" (v. 2). For Paul, joy happens when a diversity of people come together with common love and common purpose, rather than letting any other filter tear them apart.

Paul made it very clear that the primary way, the only way, to achieve this kind of harmony in community is to lean into the example of Jesus Christ. It is to let the mind of Christ be in us. We would do well to make Philippians 2:3-4 the gold standard of motive and behavior in our conversations with one another about controversial topics, whether we are talking in person or over social media.

In verses 3 and 4, Paul basically said: Do not be driven by proving yourself right. Consider the possibility that you may have something to learn from someone else. Do not let your ideology be the sole filter of your interactions with others. Look through the different interests and perspectives of people when they are different from yours. Let the very mind of Jesus Christ guide your thoughts, words, and actions.

THREE VIRTUES

Paul is telling us that there is a very clear and compelling remedy for the divisions that would tear us apart, if only all of us would choose to adhere to it. It is a remedy that comes from pursuing these three virtues: humility, curiosity, and empathy.

Imagine a world that was governed by these three virtues. Imagine a Christian community that was governed by these three ideals.

A posture of humility would remind us that we are no better and no worse than anyone else. Remember that the word *humility* comes from the Latin word *humus*, which means "ground" and "earth." To be humble means that we are connected to every other person on earth, interdependent and interconnected with them. Their welfare and well-being are intrinsically tied to yours. We survive and thrive together, as a human community beyond nations and nationalities. A grounded, earthy humility would also remind us that we are intrinsically connected to this planet, and we are responsible for its stewardship and care, not to ravage it for individual consumption, but to preserve its health for the future.

An earnest posture of humility would then lead to the value of curiosity. If we come to accept that we are connected to everyone else, then we must conclude that we do not know everything. We can remember that our perspective is not the only one, and not always even the best one or right one. That then ought to drive a spirit of curiosity. It would make us want to learn more about the world than just from within our own assumptions and biases. It means diversifying the sources of your news, puncturing the self-contained bubbles of your own social media networks, and approaching any topic with a desire to understand. It means reading a perspective that is not your own, to remember that gaining understanding of another can be as important as strengthening a conviction within yourself. This is how we grow as a civilized people. More important, it is how we grow as a faith community.

Ultimately, humility and curiosity lead to the third value, one that is perhaps in the shortest supply of all. Empathy.

Empathy is the ability to understand a situation through the outlook and experience of another person. It is to recognize that their perspective has been formed by a matrix of personal, social, and cultural forces, just like yours has. The conclusions they have made come from a deep part of who they are and who they understand themselves to be, just like yours have. Their understanding does not need to negate your own.

Empathy is risky. It requires vulnerability, transparency, and the possibility of revealing your own biases and prejudices. But ultimately, it is the way to learn to see others as fellow children of God, as people who have more in common with you than you may think.

Humility, curiosity, and empathy.

And if assuming these postures and adopting these values seem like a position of weakness to you, then that is precisely the point. To live life as God intends, we must empty ourselves in weakness, rather than amass greatness through strength.

We can do this by having the mind of Jesus, because again, Jesus did this not despite his being equal with God, but because he was God. That means that we can live with humility, curiosity, and empathy because we are made in the image of God, not despite it.

Because we are God-breathed, God-inspired, and God-created, we can be humble and obedient to God.

Because the church is born of God's spirit, and created for God's purposes, we can be more loving, more compassionate, less power-hungry, less me-centered.

Because we are God's people, not in spite of it, we can assume the servant's heart and mind.

PHILIPPIANS: THE BOOK OF JOY!

Why is living in the mind of Christ so important to Paul? Ultimately, Paul's command to live with humility, curiosity, empathy, a spirit of servanthood is rooted in Paul's central desire: to "make my joy complete."

That is such a beautiful phrase, isn't? Wouldn't it be wonderful if all of us recognized our mutual capacity to complete one another's joy? After all, this third week of Advent is often called "Gaudete" Sunday, which is the Latin word for rejoice. It is the week of joy, during a season when we are called to rejoice in the arrival of Jesus.

In the words of Paul to the Philippians, what would it be like to complete someone else's joy? Maya Angelou said, "When you wish someone joy, you wish peace, love, prosperity, health, happiness...all the good things."[3]

It is this kind of joy that is at the heart of Philippians. Paul uses the word *joy* more times in this letter to the Philippian church than in any other of his letters. And the word *rejoice* occurs more times in this book than any other book in the New Testament.

Here is just a sample:

REFLECTION QUESTIONS

1. Of these three qualities—humility, curiosity, and empathy—which do you find easiest to express? Which do you find the hardest?

2. Whom do you know who embodies these three qualities the best?

3. How might these three qualities improve your relationships with others? How might they improve communities, and the world?

Finally, my brothers and sisters, rejoice in the Lord.

To write the same things to you is not troublesome to me, and for you it is a source of steadfastness.

(Philippians 3:1 NRSVue)

Therefore, my brothers and sisters whom I love and miss, who are my joy and crown, stand firm in the Lord.

(Philippians 4:1)

Rejoice in the Lord always; again I will say, Rejoice.

(Philippians 4:4 NRSVue)

All of this is surprising, given how unjoyful Paul's circumstances were when he wrote Philippians. He wrote his most joyful letter while imprisoned. There have been a number of theories over the years about where he was imprisoned, and what he did to be sentenced there. One of the prevailing theories is that his imprisonment was based on what happened in the very last chapters of the Book of Acts, in which he was arrested for preaching the gospel in the Jerusalem temple (Acts 21). After being tried and sentenced by Jewish and Roman authorities, he wound up under house arrest in Rome. And it was here, in the most unjoyful of circumstances, that Paul was able to both experience and teach practical lessons on joy to the Christians in Philippi.

You may find joy in short supply for yourself these days. You may feel imprisoned, stuck, in a drought, or whatever word you want to use to describe the joyless state of your soul today. Or maybe, the greatest obstacle to your joy today is fear. If that's the case, then you are certainly not alone.

Just ask Mary.

MARY: FROM FEAR TO JOY

It is Mary's story that we often read on the third Sunday of Advent, and she has much to teach us about how to discover joy when we are least prone to feel joyful.

In Luke 1, when the angel Gabriel greeted Mary, his first words to her were, "Rejoice, favored one! The Lord is with you!" (v. 28). But Mary's immediate response to the angel was *not* joy. Luke tells us that she felt confused in that moment. And it is the angel who tells us what she was really feeling.

Fear.

The angel said, "Don't be afraid, Mary. God is honoring you" (v. 30).

It may be that as you approach Christmas this year, you are far from feeling the kind of joy that God wants for your life. And as you think about it, you may discover that your biggest obstacle to joy is also fear. Maybe it's fear of not having enough. Or a fear of not being enough. Or it could be fear of the next bad thing happening to you, to someone you love, or to the world.

So what can move us from fear to joy?

Just like you have probably watched *Rudolph the Red-Nosed Reindeer* at some point in your life, my hunch is that you have also seen the classic, beloved show *A Charlie Brown Christmas*. It's one of the most popular holiday shows ever produced and has been a staple for many of us ever since childhood.

If you haven't watched it yet this December, I encourage you to do so. I have come to realize just how beautifully it captures both the spirit and the message of Luke 1 and 2. When the show opens, Charlie Brown is completely joyless. He is talking to Linus, his best friend, about how he is feeling. He describes feeling unhappy even though Christmas is coming. He worries something is wrong with him because he doesn't feel how he's supposed to feel. Linus replies:

> Charlie Brown, you're the only person I know who can take a wonderful season like Christmas and turn it into a problem.

That's such a great opening scene. It may be what many of us are feeling. And it may be a sliver of what Mary was feeling. Despite the angel's good news to her, Mary was instead confused and puzzled. Fearful.

So, Charlie Brown decides to talk to another one of his friends. It's Linus's sister Lucy. You know her. She's the strong, fearless advice giver. And on occasion, the football-take-away-er. Lucy has set up her iconic therapist stand, advertising psychiatric help for 5 cents.

Charlie sits down and pays her the nickel, and then Lucy launches into this riotous exchange with him, exploring what Charlie Brown is afraid of. After they rule out hypengyophobia (fear of responsibility), ailurophasia [*sic*] (fear of cats), and a host of others, Charlie Brown confesses to feeling let down about Christmas: "Actually, Lucy, my trouble is Christmas. I just don't understand it."

Then, Lucy gives him this prescription. As it turns out, it's the same prescription that the angel gives Mary.

Lucy says, "You need involvement. You need to get involved in some real Christmas project." So, Lucy then convinces Charlie Brown to be the director of the local Christmas play.

And Charlie Brown agrees.

In Luke 1, the angel offered Mary an invitation to get involved in the most important Christmas project ever. Not to be the director of a small-town play, but to be the bearer of the greatest gift the world would ever receive. She, of all people, a young girl with no business being pregnant, would become the mother of the Messiah. The *theotokos*, as the Orthodox Church calls her. The Bearer of God.

Mary agrees.

And starting in that very moment, her emotions shift from fear to joy.

She has discovered the joy of obedience to God, and the joy of giving herself in service to others. She has pivoted away from being fixated on her internal fears and toward a life of generosity and adding value to the lives of others.

And as we draw closer toward celebrating Christmas once again, it is a pivot that you and I can make.

What can you do over these upcoming days to add value to the lives of other people? The Holy Spirit has something in mind for you to do, to impact the lives of those around you—not just by purchasing, wrapping, and giving a gift to someone, but by becoming a gift *to* them. Lucy's advice to Charlie Brown is for you as well: "You need involvement. You need to get involved in some real Christmas project."

That's the good news that the angel gave to Mary, and the opportunity to serve is what pivoted her life from fear to joy. That joy was palpable in Mary's life as she ran to meet her cousin Elizabeth, in what was an amazing scene in Luke 1. These are two people who, by all reasonable expectations, should not be pregnant. But they were.

Mary was too young. Elizabeth was too old.

Mary just got her school ID card. Elizabeth had her AARP card.

Mary wasn't old enough to drive. And Elizabeth probably shouldn't.

Mary still had her whole life ahead of her. Elizabeth couldn't imagine a whole life inside her.

Yet both of them had this one thing in common: God had gotten them involved—involved in a special project that would improve the lives of others forever beginning with Mary, who would give birth to the Messiah, and Elizabeth, who would give birth to God's messenger.

So when Mary walked into Elizabeth's house, all heaven broke loose. Elizabeth burst out in loud, joyous screaming. Her baby, John, turned her womb into a bouncy castle. She exclaimed, "God has blessed you above all women, and he has blessed the child you carry" (v. 42).

And Mary responded with some of the most powerful words in the entire Bible, and the most joyful song in the Gospels:

> *"With all my heart I glorify the Lord!*
> *In the depths of who I am I rejoice in God my savior.*
> *He has looked with favor on the low status of his servant.*
> *Look! From now on, everyone will consider me highly favored*
> *because the mighty one has done great things for me.*
> *Holy is his name.*
> *He shows mercy to everyone,*
> *from one generation to the next,*
> *who honors him as God.*

He has shown strength with his arm.
He has scattered those with arrogant thoughts and proud
inclinations.
He has pulled the powerful down from their thrones
and lifted up the lowly.
He has filled the hungry with good things
and sent the rich away empty-handed.
He has come to the aid of his servant Israel,
remembering his mercy,
just as he promised to our ancestors,
to Abraham and to Abraham's descendants forever."
(Luke 1:46-55)

Mary and Elizabeth, the two most central figures in the original Christmas story, were both transformed from fear to joy, after discovering the delight of serving others with love.

All of which finally brings us back to Charlie Brown and Linus. We were already introduced to Charlie Brown's sadness and joylessness throughout the episode. As it turns out, Linus was dealing with some issues too. Throughout the beginning of the show, the other kids, especially his sister Lucy, teased Linus for always carrying around that blue security blanket.

Well, if you've ever seen *A Charlie Brown Christmas*, you know what happens. On that stage, amid all the chaos and drama of kids trying to put on a show, the spotlight turns to Linus.

He becomes so filled with the joy of sharing the good news, the proclamation of the Christmas story in Luke 2, that his joy overcomes his fear, and he tells the story from memory, word for word, straight from the heart.

And do you know what else?

When Linus gets to the part where the angels visit the shepherds, at the very moment the angel says to the Shepherds, "Fear not"...

...Linus drops his security blanket.

That blanket had been the symbol for all he is afraid of and worried about in his life, in the face of all the teasing he got for being so anxious. But at the very moment the angels say, "Fear not," he lets it go, and then shares with the world—from memory—the good news of great joy for all people.

Friends, whatever fears are blocking your joy, take a lesson from Mary and Elizabeth, Charlie and Linus. Do not be afraid. Give yourself freely in generosity and service to others. Because Jesus has done the same for you.

And in the words of the apostle Paul to the people in Philippi: Rejoice!

A Christmas Letter from God

As we wrap up this third session, ponder again everything we've discovered from Paul's beautiful letter to the Christians in Philippi.

Despite being written in the most unjoyful of circumstances, the letter is filled with joyful exhortations. It reminds us that joy is possible in our lives, no matter what our situation in life is. Just like on The Island of Misfit Toys, we might even find ourselves in relationships and communities that seem hopeless and lost. But God has come to us in Jesus, who humbled himself not *despite* being God, but *because* he was God.

The incarnation of Jesus also models for us how we can be incarnationally present to one another, a full reflection

REFLECTION QUESTIONS

1. When has fear ever blocked your sense of joy?

2. When have you experienced the joy of giving yourself in generosity to others?

3. What is God calling you to do, to move you from fear to joy by serving others?

of Christ's self-giving love in community. Empathy reminds us to be open to other people. Curiosity reminds us to be open to other perspectives. And humility reminds us all to be open to God.

Finally, joy is possible even amid our fears. Just like Mary (and all the main characters of the birth narratives) experienced fear at the outset of their encounter with God, joy comes when we see ourselves as part of God's wider plan of redemption for the world. We are not alone, and we are part of a greater purpose. Giving ourselves over to God's work in service to others is a source of full, lasting joy.

So with these lessons in mind, what might it look like for you to receive a special letter of your own, from the God who meets you in your situation and offers you joy?

My Child,

I know you have difficult memories that are hard to shake. Times when you felt sorry for yourself, or hurt by others, or lost and confused about your life. You have been through times that have felt like an imprisonment, trapped in the recurring messages of heartbreak and hopelessness that you cannot seem to escape.

There is a lot about humanity today that is less than the ideal that I intend for it. But no one is a lost cause forever. No one is a permanent misfit. You certainly are not. And that is all the more reason that I came to earth in Jesus. Through him, you see me. And in him, I fully identify with you. I became human, and I experienced everything, including death. But it meant that you and I could have a new relationship together, one in which you can see yourself as my precious child, and you can have the possibility of deep and lasting joy.

And here's another thing: because of Jesus, you can also have joy-filled relationships with others. Practice empathy. Just like I can fully identify with your sufferings, be open to the perspective of other people. Practice curiosity. I have given you the amazing capacity to learn, to grow, and to use your intelligence. Be open to new ideas—even if they seem at odds with what you know. Most of all, practice humility. Here's a newsflash: you aren't the center of the universe. But you know the One who is. And I am here to show you how to be at peace with others and yourself.

Oh, and don't be afraid. I know you've heard me say that, over and over again, to many people, including you. But really. Put your hand in mine. Let's take a walk, one day at a time, step by step, and I'll guide you through life. Don't skip ahead of me, and don't lag behind. Just you and me, in perfect cadence. Surrender yourself in obedience to what I ask of you. Let your fears go, and replace them with trust in me.

Then, do you know what will happen? Joy will happen!

That's what I want for you!

God

CHAPTER 4

FULLY DIVINE

Peace through Christ

CHAPTER 4

Fully Divine

Peace through Christ

The Son is the image of the invisible God,
  the one who is first over all creation,

Because all things were created by him:
  both in the heavens and on the earth,
  the things that are visible and the things that are invisible.
    Whether they are thrones or powers,
    or rulers or authorities,
  all things were created through him and for him.

He existed before all things,
  and all things are held together in him.

He is the head of the body, the church,
who is the beginning,
  the one who is firstborn from among the dead
  so that he might occupy the first place in everything.

Because all the fullness of God was pleased to live in him,
  and he reconciled all things to himself through him—
  whether things on earth or in the heavens.
    He brought peace through the blood of his cross.
                                    (Colossians 1:15-20)

There's a term in psychology called the reminiscence bump. It's the theory that the music you listened to when you were in your teens and twenties is etched in your memory and stays with you your whole life. During late adolescence and early adulthood, our brain's memory systems are at their most efficient. (How's that for sobering news?) That means that, if you are above the age of thirty or so, remembering lyrics was easier then than now.

But more important, it is during that formative period of our lives when our identity and personhood most take shape. So the music we listen to as teens and young adults bears an intrinsic link to critical and memorable events in our personal development: the significant choices we were making, the long-term relationships we were forming, the first glimpses of independence we were experiencing, and the cultural, political, and religious beliefs we were choosing to view the world.

So the reminiscence bump phenomena suggest that when you listen to that music now, you can not only remember the lyrics, you can remember who you were and who you are.

It's certainly true for me.

Play the theme song to *Mister Rogers' Neighborhood* and I can sing every word, picturing myself sitting in front of the television as a youngster.

Have me listen to the theme song from *Greatest American Hero* and I can sing every word, and I can picture my third-grade friend David as we made replica Greatest American Hero action figures out of pipe cleaners and construction paper.

If I hear Billy Joel's "We Didn't Start the Fire," I can picture myself hanging out with my college buddies in our freshman dorm room.

And don't get me started on "Never Gonna Give You Up" by Rick Astley. I feel like my young adult years were filled with one rickroll after another.

It is the songs of our youth that stick with us longer than any other.

Paul's Letter to the Colossians is written to Christians in adolescence. Paul had never visited the city personally, nor had he met the people to whom he was writing. A fellow missionary named Epaphras started that church, so everything Paul knew about the Colossians was secondhand.

But he did know this. He knew that the Christians in Colossae were in a formative—and vulnerable—stage of their faith. They had just become followers of Jesus, and therefore they had just begun to face the pressures and temptations of the culture around them. He knew there were many forces that would veer them away from their commitment to Jesus. So if you read Colossians—which shouldn't take long, since it's only four chapters long—it reads like a parent giving their adolescent child some advice on how to experience the world for themselves.

So it should be no surprise that in the first chapter of Colossians, Paul teaches them a song. It would be a song that he hoped would stick with them through the adolescence of their faith and provide a kind of "reminiscence bump" for the rest of their lives.

What we find in Colossians 1:15-20 is apparently one of the earliest Christian hymns sung about Jesus Christ. We don't know how the melody went, or how catchy the hook was, but we do know the lyrics.

> *The Son is the image of the invisible God,*
> > *the one who is first over all creation,*
>
> *Because all things were created by him:*
> > *both in the heavens and on the earth,*
> > *the things that are visible and the things that are invisible.*
> > > *Whether they are thrones or powers,*
> > > *or rulers or authorities,*
> > > *all things were created through him and for him.*
>
> *He existed before all things,*
> > *and all things are held together in him.*
>
> *He is the head of the body, the church,*
> *who is the beginning,*
> > *the one who is firstborn from among the dead*
> > *so that he might occupy the first place in everything.*
>
> *Because all the fullness of God was pleased to live in him,*
> > *and he reconciled all things to himself through him—*
> > *whether things on earth or in the heavens.*
> > > *He brought peace through the blood of his cross.*

Paul knew this was an important song to embed into the foundation of the early Christians' faith, so that they could carry it with them as they passed the faith down through the generations. And as we look at this song through the lens of Christmas and the incarnation of Jesus, we discover some important aspects of Christian belief and practice that we shouldn't forget either.

Let's walk through the song a few lines at a time.

"The Son is the image of the invisible God."

The first-century Greco-Roman world was shaped by a polytheistic worldview, in which there were multiple gods at work in the function and order of the universe. But like many of the earliest Christians, Paul believed in one true, supreme Creator God, rooted in his monotheistic, Jewish upbringing.

But this first line doesn't stop there. Paul makes a crucial connection between God and Jesus, to say that they are one and the same. Jesus is the "image" of the "invisible" God.

All throughout the Old Testament, God was revealed to the Israelites in very visible ways. In the Creation story, God hovered over the waters of chaos and walked in the garden searching for Adam and Eve. In the Exodus, God was visible through a burning bush, audible through a voice calling out to Moses, and present in the form of a billowing cloud by day and a fiery pillar at night.

But by the time we get to the period of the Greeks and Romans, the biblical record changes in the way people experienced God. When Jesus was born, he became the complete and ultimate revelation of God to humanity.

In saying that Jesus was the "image" of the "invisible" God, Paul was saying that anything and everything we would ever want to know about who God is can be seen in ways that we can most directly relate and understand—through a human being, much like us.

Consider this truth in light of Matthew's story of the birth of Jesus. His is the only Gospel to mention Herod, the king of Judea and appointee of the Roman Empire. When he heard news of Jesus's birth, he considered it a threat to his throne and a threat to the empire. Even Herod, with all his paranoia and addiction to power, saw Jesus as one who had come with divine power.

Fast forward about four hundred years after Jesus. The faith of the early Christian church had been centered on Easter, and the story of the cross, the Crucifixion, and the resurrection of Jesus. Eventually, the church began to take an interest in the Nativity story as a way of asserting that Jesus was not only greater than the panoply of Greco-Roman gods but was also greater than all earthly rulers who had claimed divine authority.

That is when the church began to emphasize the Nativity stories in the Gospels. The Greeks had claimed that Alexander the Great was born from a human mother impregnated by the Greek god Zeus. But Christians were able to raise them one further, claiming that Jesus was born of the virgin Mary by an immaculate conception. Romans believed that when Augustus Caesar was born, a star shone bright in the sky. Christians took it one more step, to say there wasn't just a bright shiny star when Jesus was born, there was also a sky full of singing angels.

For the early church, the origin story of Jesus underscored the message of Colossians: Jesus was the image of the invisible God, the definitive Savior of the world, and the Lord of the universe.

But there's one other aspect to the birth of Jesus that sets him apart from every other origin story of other gods and divine rulers in history.

Notice that in the story of the birth of Jesus, every single person who encounters the baby Jesus had their life transformed.

Joseph was transformed from someone who felt confused, afraid, and betrayed into someone who put family first, and was willing to protect them at all costs.

The shepherds were transformed from being average workers into heralds of good news for the world.

Zechariah and Elizabeth went from being an aging, disheartened couple to bearing the one who would prepare the way of the Lord.

And then there is Mary, who was just an ordinary young girl from an obscure, backwater village, who simply said yes to God and gave birth to hope for the world.

The story of Jesus's birth is not just some divinized birth story of some great earthly power who came from the heavens. It is also a rebirth story, of people who were reborn and renewed when they encountered this baby Jesus. It is about how their lives were transformed from hopelessness into hope, from fear into courage, and from darkness into light.

The great Christian mystic Meister Eckhart said it more eloquently than I ever could: "[Christ's birth] is always happening. And yet, if it does not occur in me, how could it help me? Everything depends on that."[1]

Christmas is not just the story of the birth of Jesus. It can be a story of rebirth for you.

"The first over all creation."

Other translations of this text say that Jesus was the "firstborn" of all creation. But this is not about birth order, since Jesus was, in fact, God's only son (John 3:16). Nor does it mean that Jesus was created, since this Scripture (and John 1) affirm that Jesus and God are one.

To call Jesus the first over all Creation means that the second person of the Trinity was there at the time of Creation, and is therefore evident in all creation. When we look at the beauty and mystery of the world around us, it points to the wonder and majesty of Jesus Christ. And when we look at Jesus, we discover God's presence, activity, and intention in the world. In the words of Eugene Peterson's translation of this verse, "We look at this Son and see God's original purpose in everything created" (MSG).

That means that when Jesus was born, God became human, and the Creator became the created. This was not simply a sculptor chiseling away at marble to create a statue, or a seamstress stitching together a fashion statement, or an author typing out a masterpiece of fiction. This was the creator *becoming the created itself*, so that in looking at Jesus, you see the presence and power of God.

But then the lyrics become even more marvelous.

> *Because all things were created by him:*
> > *both in the heavens and on the earth,*
> > *the things that are visible and the things that are invisible.*
> > > *Whether they are thrones or powers,*
> > > *or rulers or authorities,*
> > *all things were created through him and for him.*
> > > > *(Colossians 1:16)*

REFLECTION QUESTIONS

1. What songs constitute your "reminiscence bump"? When you hear these songs, what do you recall about your younger self?

2. What songs come to mind when you think about the adolescent stage of your faith? Were there hymns or songs that you associate with the early days of your belief?

3. In what ways has your life been transformed by Jesus, like the characters in the Christmas narrative?

Take a look at that last r: not only did God the Creator become the created, but all things were also created *through* Jesus and *for* Jesus. That means that in some amazing and wondrous way, when Jesus was born, all of God's creative power and imagination assumed human form. In that infant child, in that tiny collection of freshly formed muscles and organs, skin cells and nerve endings, brain waves and heartbeats, was born the very conduit through which all of creation came into being.

When Jesus took his first breath, he took into his lungs the very oxygen molecules that he first set into motion. When he first opened his eyes, he was flooded with the very light waves that he spoke into being on day one of Creation. When he took in nourishment from his mother, he was receiving sustenance given with the same generosity that he provided for countless generations.

In that infant Jesus was all the creative agency, imagination, and history that this universe has ever seen, and will ever see.

"He existed before all things..."

Now, if your mind isn't blown yet, or if you're scratching your head trying to make sense of all this (which is quite understandable—this is astounding stuff to ponder), let's do a bit of a visualization exercise. It is a mental journey that can help us see how the God of the universe is fully revealed in the incarnation of Jesus and the profound difference it can make in how we see ourselves.

It is a journey that I would characterize in three movements: infinite, intimate, and incarnate.

First, infinite. Pondering the vastness of the universe fills us with a mind-blowing sense of infinity, doesn't it? It is hard for us to even imagine what is at the edge of the universe or beyond, because as big as the universe is, it continues to expand. Even light waves emitted from the stars are expanding, into an infrared wavelength beyond what the naked eye can see. That's the whole premise of the James Webb Space Telescope—and as powerful as it is, we can only see a portion of a universe that some estimate to be 93-94 billion light years wide. Our minds can't grasp a size that big.

But here's something else that is equally mind-blowing. There is not only a sense of the infinite when we look out. There is also infinity when we look within. In his book *Fundamentals*, Frank Wilczek writes that as hard as it is to imagine the number of stars in the universe, there are even more atoms in the human body. It is ten octillion, which is ten followed by twenty-eight zeroes.[2] That is what is inside you. It is what makes up who you are, a collection of protons, neutrons, and electrons.

There is literally a universe inside you.

And just as there is a limit to what we can see beyond the edge of space, there is a limit to what we can see inside the atom. The further down we look, we get into the vast, unknown, unpredictability of quarks, Higgs boson particles, quantum mechanics, and a reality that is infinitely small and unknowable.

So whether we ponder the universe through Galileo's telescope, or ponder the infinitesimal through Antonie van Leeuwenhoek's microscope, we reach the limits of our understanding. Either way, a sense of the infinite offers this gift to us: a sense of wonder, awe, and an embrace of the mysteries of the world beyond our comprehension.

Okay, so given the vastness of the universe around us and within us, let's take the next step in our visualization exercise.

Intimate. As vast as the universe is out there, and within you, here is something to remember: we are all intimately connected in this grand cosmos.

Of the most abundant elements in the universe, four of the top six are nitrogen, carbon, oxygen, and hydrogen (which is by far the most plentiful element). Now, do you want to know what the top four elements are that make up your body? Yep, the exact same ones. Carbon, oxygen, nitrogen, and hydrogen. What that means is that the very material that makes up your body makes up the same building blocks that God used to create the farthest planets and stars on the edge of the universe. The very atoms that were created 13.8 billion years ago are part of your body right now. No wonder you feel old!

We are made of the stuff of the stars. You and I are made of stardust.

Here's something else. The very oxygen molecules you are breathing right now have been around since the time of the dinosaurs. The components that make up the nitrogen molecule in your blood? They may have arrived from a star millions of years ago.

This is all to say that as infinite and daunting as the universe is, there is an intimacy in knowing that you and I are connected by the same material, governed by the same forces of gravity and electromagnetism, and created by the very God who became human in Jesus. The infinity of the universe might make us feel small, but the intimacy of its materials helps us not feel so alone.

This all leads us to the final movement of this visualization exercise.

Incarnate. Throughout history, many religious philosophers believed in the idea of deism, which is that God is nothing more than an impersonal clockmaker, who set forth the mechanics of creation and stepped away from it to leave it on its own. But as Christian people, we believe that God is not distant. God is both present and immanent in all things and beyond all things.

We can know God by interacting with this marvelous world.

And when God chose to be revealed to us in the most vivid way, you know what God chose to do. God entered the universe as a human being...composed of stardust just like you and me. God showed us through Jesus the infinite glory of God in the most intimate of ways: by becoming incarnate to us. And God showed us how we can be an incarnate sense of love to one another.

"...and all things are held together in him."

If I were to pick one line from this whole hymn in Colossians 1 to ask you to commit to memory, it would be this one in verse 17.

It is no coincidence that this line is in the very center of the entire hymn, because it suggests that Jesus Christ can be the center that can hold everything in your life together.

All things are held together in him. Jesus is the only center that can hold.

I serve a multisite congregation in Tampa, Florida. Not far from our church campuses is the Port of Tampa, from which massive cargo and cruise ships sail in and out each day. These massive ships are driven by huge turbines that spin blades at incredibly high speeds and push out water to make the ship go.

You can envision in your mind what these turbines look like: large fan blades that are connected to a central shaft, which is connected to the engines. The shaft spins, the blades rotate, and the ship goes.

Now here's what's interesting: theoretically speaking, there is a line that runs down the center line of that shaft, from tip to tip, that stays perfectly fixed, immobile, regardless of how fast those blades are rotating. Think about it. Even though those blades are rotating at amazingly high speeds, that center line stays fixed. And if there were any vibration, any motion whatsoever in the center line of that shaft, it will break, the blades will fly apart, and the ship won't move.

What matters most is what's in the center.

Your life has a lot of rotating fan blades. Each of us has chaos swirling in our lives. There's not a single exception among us. One personal crisis after another, uncertain futures, and unsteady times.

And we will try anything to hold it all together, looking for a center that is steady. We look for ways to distract us and divert us from all the chaos, but those makeshift centers will not hold. Some of us will try to find significance and meaning through our careers, our accomplishments, our possessions, or even our children. Some of us will pursue strategies that wind up causing us even more chaos and harm.

Paul is very clear in this hymn: Jesus is the only center of your life that will hold. He's been with you since your earliest days, and through the adolescence of your faith. He's more powerful than any ruler or kingdom in the world, and wants to be your Lord. He's the center that remains fixed through any hardship and will hold amid any chaos.

And all that's required is for you to put Jesus in the center of your life.

A full commitment to Jesus is what Paul is thinking of. You wouldn't get this from any other guy. Paul just wants to tell you how he's feeling. Paul just wants to make you understand that Jesus is...

> Never gonna give you up,
> Never gonna let you down.[3]

(Sorry, I couldn't help it.)

We come now to the final line in this Colossians hymn, and we see how it all fits together. Because all things are in Christ, and because Christ is in all things, and because we are part of the creation that Christ has both created and drawn into himself, we are part of God's greatest work in history: reconciliation.

Another word for that is *peace*, which is our final key word for Advent.

Because of the Incarnation, Crucifixion, and resurrection of Jesus, there is one thing that is even more infinite than

REFLECTION QUESTIONS

1. When you consider Jesus, what do you come to know about God?

2. How does pondering the infinity and vastness of the universe expand your view of Jesus?

3. How will you make Jesus the center of your life?

the stars of the universe and the atoms in your body. It is the capacity and power of love that pulls us together, so that we can forge relationships of peace with one another and all of creation.

Because of Christ's reconciling work, we can experience the wonder, awe, and majesty of God's creation. That means that as big as this universe is, we don't have to feel alone. God has given us the gift of one another to enjoy it, and to take care of it.

Paul's song in Colossians was meant to be more than merely memorable for those early Christians. It was meant to be formative, so that whenever they would face the pressures and temptations to believe and act in a way contrary to the way of Jesus, they would recall this song, and the meaning behind it.

Of course, hearing the song and *remembering* it are two very different things—even for songs that are part of our "reminiscence bump."

REMEMBERING THE LYRICS

Not long ago I had both my daughters in town as we made final preparations for them to start their new school years. One night, the girls asked me to join in on a game they kind of made up called "Blind Karaoke." Apparently, it's a thing on social media.

Unlike regular karaoke, where you sing words that are on a screen, in blind karaoke you sing with your back to the screen, and sing all the words from memory. The catch is that these are songs that you are supposed to know well because you have claimed them to be among your favorite songs over the past year.

This started with Spotify users, who challenged one another to sing blind karaoke to the songs that were their most listened to songs over the past twelve months. Supposedly, you have listened to these songs so much, over and over again, that you should know all the lyrics. Right?

Well, needless to say, I failed miserably. From the latest Christian hits to the songs of my youth in the 1970s and 1980s, I found myself doing more humming than actual singing. The girls did much better, mostly due to their love of Taylor Swift, but they screwed up enough times to send the three of us into delirious laughter.

The only song I got right, 100 percent? A Disney song. It was one the girls and I used to sing in the car over and over again when they were little, from the film *Mulan*. It's titled "I'll Make a Man Out of You." So that night, when I sang the line "Did they send me daughters when I asked for sons?" the girls yelled, "So *that's* a line you remember?"

What I learned from blind karaoke is this spiritual principle: When it comes to singing, we can't do it blindly, and we can't do it alone. We need to be in the company of others, to sing, pray, and worship together, and to allow the Word of Christ to dwell in us richly.

That is what Paul intends for the church in Colossae and for all of us: a reminiscence bump, an invitation to come together to remember that this Jesus, the firstborn of all creation, the incarnate presence of God and the fullness of humanity, has been with the Colossians from the beginning. Because if they could remember this song, and remember the *meaning* of this song, then no matter what changes and challenges occurred in the future, this song could always bring them back to a sense of assurance and certainty about God.

May that be the same for you and me. This week's reading from Colossians might serve as a reminiscence bump to remind you of the early, formative moments of your own faith, of your earliest inklings of who Jesus Christ was to you, and remind you of the times when you first began to sense the presence of God at work in your life. It is the activity of prevenient grace, as Methodists call it.

Reminisce with me. If you were raised in the Christian faith, you may have tender memories of hearing your parents read you Bible stories or your grandparents praying out loud. How about a Sunday school teacher who taught using a flannel board or led you in songs like "Jesus Loves the Little Children"?

You might recall the summer camp where you lifted a hand to accept Jesus into your heart, or the church building where you knelt for your confirmation, or the moment you held in your hands the first Bible you ever owned.

Some of your memories may be deeply internal. Like the time you felt alone and reached out to God for the first time for a sense of companionship and hope. Or when you felt afraid and sensed the comfort of God in your heart. Or when you felt the wonder and awe of God in nature and realized that something out there is so much bigger than you imagined.

But we can't help realizing how much has changed in our lives since those early years, huh? As time has gone by, your younger days of innocence and wonder have been etched with trauma and hardship that you could not have expected. You may have wandered off for a bit in a world of competing ideas and belief systems, even going through patches of doubt, or skepticism or disbelief. You may even be going through that now. There may have been times when you have experienced harm from other churches in your past, and you are more wary about the faith than you were before.

Well, Paul would say to each of us today: welcome back and welcome home. He would invite us to listen to this song, and remember that even since the earliest, most tender days of our faith journey, you've never been alone. God has been with you, and God is with you still.

Remember who you are in Christ, and how you are connected to all creation because of what God has done in Jesus. Because it is far too easy to forget it, especially during Advent and the Christmas season.

And if we do, we will miss the awe and wonder of being in Christ.

DON'T MISS IT

In a radio episode of *The Moth* storytelling hour, writer and humorist Andy Christie told a story of a memorable Christmas many years ago when he was eight years old.[4] He and his older brother, Artie, were visiting his father's apartment in New York City one Christmas morning when their dad presented them with gifts that were, in Andy's words, "freakishly unequal."

The difference in sheer scale between his little gift and his brother's massive gift had little eight-year-old Andy instantly weepy. He was standing there, with his standard, green-and-red-striped package, while his twelve-year-old brother, Artie, had to literally *walk around* his present in order to start opening it.

His brother's gift was the kind of present that was so enormous, magical, and shapeless that it was almost saying, "No box could ever hold the wonder inside there," as if someone "threw a Santa Claus–style tarp on top of a pile of puppies or something."

His brother opened his present first. It was a forty- or fifty-gallon fish tank, with all the accessories. Rainbow gravel, bubbling scuba diver, plastic seaweed, treasure chest, filter, stand, everything but the fish.

Andy opened his present, and it was a book. Just an ordinary-looking book.

It had a black cover, and it basically looked like a textbook. He opened it, and it was filled with the weirdest pictures he'd ever seen: ornately drawn, baroque-style artwork with some of the most disturbing images he had ever seen in his eight years of life. There were devils with giant bat wings, swinging severed human heads, men and women on fire, none of them clothed. Just horrible pictures, none of them in color.

And when he tore himself away from the pictures to look at the words, he realized that the book was written in Italian.

To his dad's credit, he knew that Andy liked books, and that he liked to draw, so his dad put some thought into it. But he did give him a book with pictures that he found unsettling and words he could not read.

So Andy was disappointed.

You and I could probably relate to young Andy, couldn't we? He was judging the merits of his gift based on volume and mass alone.

Andy looked at his book, then glanced over at Artie's veritable Sea World theme park, and just started sobbing. Artie, on the other hand, showed very little interest in the aquarium. He stood there with one of the plastic tubes in his hands. One end in his mouth, the other end blowing air into one of his ears. He didn't care about fish tanks.

But Andy did, if for no other reason than his brother had one and he didn't.

Artie, on the other hand, took a look at his little brother's new book, saw the grotesque pictures, and, being twelve, was much more intrigued by them.

He said to Andy, "Wanna trade?"

So they did.

If we care to admit it, our anticipation of Christmas often exceeds the payoff of Christmas. Maybe it's because our excitement is based on standards of volume and mass. It's as if we have been setting ourselves up over these past few weeks to experience voluminous happiness or massive contentment, for at least on Christmas Day. We do this to ourselves every December, only to discover sometimes that when we set our expectations that high, we feel like when December 26 rolls around, we sense that we've missed something in the end.

Even Luke's Gospel sets up this disparity of expectations. Look at the first two sentences in his birth narrative, the part we often skip right past: "In those days Caesar Augustus declared that everyone throughout the empire should be enrolled in the tax lists. This first enrollment occurred when Quirinius governed Syria" (2:1-2).

The emperor, the governor, the Roman rulers—their contentment and peace were based on volume and mass: the size of the population, the projected income from taxes, the anticipated expansion of the empire. Their expectations were even bigger than a fifty-gallon fish tank.

But Luke then pans the camera away from the aquarium of the Roman Empire and zooms in on the much smaller gift. It was presented by a lowly young couple from an inconspicuous town called Nazareth. Just a humble man and his pregnant wife, stumbling into Bethlehem to be counted as just another number.

And if we're honest, there is a part of us every year with such Augustus-sized expectations for Christmas that we miss the smaller, more subtle gift this season can bring.

So the message here is just three simple words.

Don't miss it.

Don't miss the blessings of God evident in your life, and at work in the world—blessings that you will miss if you look for them in more grandiose standards. If the Christmas story tells us anything, it is that the peace, joy, hope, and love that we have been anticipating comes in smaller, more subtle, but much more impactful moments.

So don't miss them.

Here are just a few examples, some of them inspired by one of my favorite writers, Anne Lamott.[5]

Number 1. Don't miss a chance to look up into the sky. I mean, literally. Give yourself more opportunities to look up, especially on Christmas Eve. Remember the shepherds. They were the first ones to know about the birth of Jesus, maybe because they were the only ones looking up, while the townsfolk were busy doing the kinds of things that we townsfolk always do. Find some moments to breathe fresh air, look up into the clouds, the sunset, the sunrise, the stars. It will give you perspective. Anne Lamott once said the reason you can trap bees in a jar is because they never look up. Instead, they are always bumping into invisible walls because they don't look above them. So don't miss a chance to look up.

Number 2. Don't miss the chance to forgive; that includes forgiving yourself. Grace is spiritual WD-40, Lamott says. It's like water wings. And despite what you have done, or what others have done to you, grace never goes away. God's love really is for all people, and God loves you and me as much as God loves Vladimir Putin and Kim Jong Un. Earth is forgiveness school, Lamott says. So sometime in the coming days, you will have a chance to forgive someone else. And you may have a chance to forgive yourself. Don't miss it.

Number 3. Don't miss the chance to say I love you, I'm sorry, and thank you. These three phrases are easy to say, but difficult to really mean. I love you says you matter to me. I'm sorry says my actions matter to you. Thank you says that our relationship matters to us. Say these three things in equal measure to one another in the days ahead, and it's like opening an exciting present in your relationship together.

Number 4. Don't miss the chance to sing. Despite all the confusion and hardship in our lives and in the world, God can always put a melody in our hearts. Find a song that brings you joy. Better yet, find a song that adds more joy and beauty in the world, and claim it. Sing it. Sing it in front of others if you dare. They'll let you know if you can keep going. But either way, do as John Wesley advised, and sing it lustily. Find that song. Don't miss it.

Finally, Number 5. Don't miss the chance to see Jesus. He's here. In a weird way, we've been anticipating the coming of someone who has always been with us—and never really left. That's the paradox of Advent and Christmas. But in a way, all truth is paradoxical, isn't it? The greatest truths, the ones we can bank our lives on, are the ones that both make perfect sense and are still hard to believe. That's especially true in how we might see Jesus.

Matthew said we could find him in the faces of the poor, the hungry, and the sick. Luke said we could find Jesus in the oppressed, the downtrodden, and the underdog. Mark said we could find him on the cross, where we discover our sins on his body instead of our own. John said we could find him in the truth of God's love, staring us in the mirror, when we acknowledge just how much God loves you and me and all people everywhere.

Consider this list of five not just my gift to you, but also just a starter set. My hope is that you will add to this list for yourself, and each time when you discover a blessing from God that you might otherwise miss, it will be like opening another present under the tree. One that you would have otherwise missed.

All of this brings us back to the story of writer and producer Andy Christie and his Christmas gift swap with his brother, Artie. The presents, it turns out, were given to them by their father while he was a superintendent of that apartment complex. It was a boarding house for single men in New York City. Every once in a while, for whatever reason, a tenant would leave all their belongings behind, either because of a sudden move or death. It was not unusual for their father to pick through the belongings of the departed tenants, put them in a sack, and bring them downstairs to his apartment, where they would be presented to his boys under a Christmas tree or next to a birthday cake.

That's what happened on that Christmas morning, in which Andy traded the book for the aquarium. Andy enjoyed his newly acquired fish tank for a few days, before realizing how much work it involved. Over time, the glass got covered in green slime, the fish didn't make it, and the whole operation wound up in the trash out back, just a few weeks after Christmas. Artie, on the other hand, held on to the book, never really paying much attention to it, and left it in his room.

Years later, when they were much older, and after their father died, Andy and Artie went back to their dad's apartment to clean out their old bedrooms. The next morning, Artie called Andy.

Artie said, "Hey, have you ever heard of a nineteenth-century artist named Gustave Dorè?"

"Yes, I have in fact," Andy replied, because his childhood love for drawing had led him to attend art school.

"Well, have you ever heard of *Dante's Inferno*?"

"I have."

It turned out the old book was an 1863 copy of Gustave Dore's illustrated masterpiece of *Dante's Divine Comedy*, what book people call a "first impression with book plates." And it was worth a lot more than a fish tank.

Don't miss it, friends. This Christmas, and over the days to come, don't get fixated on a superficial experience of joy based on mass and volume. The blessings of God are in the smaller moments, the ones we might overlook. Look for the little things.

Merry Christmas, friends.

And don't miss it.

THE CHRISTMAS LETTERS

Throughout this journey, we have discovered insights into the Incarnation from some of the earliest witnesses in Christian history. Each one has helped us to see how the arrival of Jesus into the world has forever shaped our view of God, ourselves, and our relationship with God.

Romans showed us the beauty of the long view, both as a remembrance of the past and the work of God into the future. Just as the birth of Jesus was part of a grand story that stretched from the beginning of time and into eternity, God is working in your life the same way. Remember what God has done in your life, and give thanks. Claim the promised future that God is unfolding in your life, and don't give up.

The epistles of John help us to see the incarnation of Jesus as a fulfillment of God's intended creation (Genesis), a light for us amid the darkness (the Gospel of John), and an embodiment of God's love for all people (1 John). Whenever you are feeling lost and confused, Jesus is there for you through the fellowship of others, as you surround one another in relationships of both love and truth.

Philippians points us to the way of Jesus, who embodied humility, curiosity, and empathy. These are important antidotes to the brokenness and division that plague our culture today. By becoming fully human, and obedient to the mission to which God had called him, he showed us how to offer ourselves in service to others. The Incarnation therefore gives us a pathway to both servanthood and joy, as we fully live into our potential and make a difference in the world.

And here, in Colossians, we see the incarnation of Christ's glorious divinity. He was there since the beginning, as Creator of all things. He lives in us still, cocreating a new future for each of us who calls him Lord. As we ponder the wonder of the infant Jesus, we see in his face the glory of all that has been created, and we even discover the potential of new creation within ourselves. We see in Jesus all that has been, will be, and is becoming, moment by moment.

Hopefully, this journey has expanded your view of the impact of the Incarnation. While we most often associate Jesus's birth with the classic infancy narratives in the Gospels, these letters show us that even before those stories were written down, and as they were being circulated in oral tradition, the significance of Jesus's arrival on earth was already being pondered by the earliest Christian communities.

The question for each of us today is, What difference does this make? How will you make the story of Christmas more than a tale that is recounted from our history, but instead an ongoing, lived reality that shapes lives and transforms communities?

How will you receive these letters of old and make them alive again in your life?

GOD'S CHRISTMAS LETTER TO YOU

My Child,

There is so much wonder and awe that I wish for you to experience this Christmas. Soon, you will be joining with loved ones and friends to celebrate the birth of my Son. I am eager to see your face brim with joy as you light the candles, sing the carols, and hear the ancient stories from the Gospels that I have shared for generations.

Pay special attention this year to the deeper meaning of the rituals of Christmas. You're not just celebrating a story from long ago. You are remembering that in Jesus, I have always been with you, and I always will be. His infant body contained the origin of the cosmos, and the source of my infinite love for you. He was—and still is—the best and fullest reflection of who I am. When you look at Jesus, you see all of me—my presence, my power, my grace. All of it.

I know this is hard to fathom. I created the human mind to be imaginative and adept at learning new things. But you have limits in what you can understand. That's where your faith steps in. It allows you to stretch out your hand, so that I can take yours into mine. And then I'll help you sense the everyday wonder of my presence all around you, and within you.

You'll discover hope, rooted in all I have done for you in the past, which will guide you into even the most unsettled, unknown parts of your future.

You'll discover love, incarnate in Jesus and in your relationships with others, reminding you that you are not alone.

You'll discover joy, immeasurable and available, that will enable you to serve others with empathy, curiosity, and humility.

And you'll find peace, in the midst of even your deepest brokenness, because I am here, reconciling you and all things to myself.

This Christmas, may you remember more than just a story about Jesus's birth. May you discover new life in me, each and every day, with eyes wide open. That is my wish for you.

Merry Christmas!

God

REFLECTION QUESTIONS

1. How will you make the Christmas story more than something you remember, but instead something you live out?

2. What will you do to make sure you don't miss what God wants to reveal to you this Christmas?

3. What key insights have you learned from this Advent journey? How will you apply them all year round?

NOTES

Chapter 2

1 Warren W. Wiersbe, *On Being a Leader for God* (Grand Rapids, MI: Baker Books, 2011), 39.

2 Timothy Keller and Kathy Keller, *The Meaning of Marriage: Facing the Complexities of Commitment with the Wisdom of God* (New York: Riverhead Books, 2013), 44.

3 W. Reginald Ward and Richard P. Heitzenrater, eds., *The Works of John Wesley: Journals and Diaries I* (1735-38) (Nashville: Abingdon Press, 1984), 18:249-50.

4 Barna Group, "Christians: More Like Jesus or Pharisees?" June 3, 2013, https://www.barna.com/research/christians-more-like-jesus-or-pharisees/.

5 David Gushee, *Introducing Christian Ethics: Core Convictions for Christians Today* (Canton, MI: Front Edge Publishing, 2022), 226.

6 Gushee, *Introducing Christian Ethics*, 221.

Chapter 3

1 Sean J. Westwood, Shanto Iyengar, Stefaan Walgrave, Rafael Leonisio, Luis Miller, Oliver Strijbis, "The Tie that Divides: Cross-national Evidence of the Primacy of Partyism," European Journal of Political Research, August 11, 2017, https://ejpr.onlinelibrary.wiley.com/doi/abs/10.1111/1475-6765.12228.

2 Will Willimon, "Will Willimon: One in Christ," Day 1, October 1, 2017, https://day1.org/weekly-broadcast/5d9b820ef71918cdf200416b/will_willimon_one_in_christ.

3 Abby Phillip, "52 Tweeted Messages of Wisdom from Maya Angelou," *The Washington Post*, May 28, 2014, https://www.washingtonpost.com/news/arts-and-entertainment/wp/2014/05/28/52-tweeted-messages-of-wisdom-from-maya-angelou/.

Chapter 4

1 *Meister Eckhart: A Modern Translation*, trans. Raymond Bernard Blakney (New York: Harper & Row, 1941), 95.

2 Frank Wilczek, *Fundamentals: Ten Keys to Reality* (New York: Penguin, 2021) 14.

3 "Never Gonna Give You Up," sung by Rick Astley. Songwriters: Peter Alan Waterman / Matthew James Aitken / Michael Stock. Never Gonna Give You Up lyrics © All Boys Music Ltd., Sids Songs Ltd., Mike Stock Publishing Limited.

4 Andy Christie, "The Ghost of Christmas Presents," The Moth, December 24, 2013, https://themoth.org/stories/the-ghost-of -christmas-presents. Accessed June 1, 2024.

5 Anne Lamott, "12 Truths I Learned from Life and Writing," TED2017, April 2017, https://www.ted.com/talks/anne _lamott_12_truths_i_learned_from_life_and_writing?hasSummary =true&language=en.

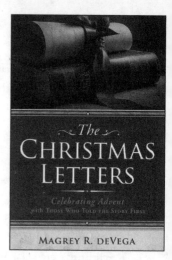